Xmas 1943

With love and Good Wishes

From

Mary Charlotte

BORDER BY-WAYS
& LOTHIAN LORE

a

DRYBURGH, WEST DOORWAY

BORDER BY-WAYS
& LOTHIAN LORE

BY

T. RATCLIFFE BARNETT

NEW AND ENLARGED EDITION

THE MORAY PRESS
EDINBURGH & LONDON

THE MORAY PRESS
126 PRINCES STREET, EDINBURGH
182 HIGH HOLBORN, LONDON, W.C.1

FIRST EDITION, MAY 1925
REPRINTED, JULY 1925
FIRST CHEAP EDITION, 1933
NEW & ENLARGED EDITION, 1937

PRINTED IN SCOTLAND
BY THE DUNEDIN PRESS LIMITED, EDINBURGH
AND BOUND BY
WILLIAM HUNTER & SONS, EDINBURGH
FOR
GRANT & MURRAY LIMITED
126 PRINCES STREET, EDINBURGH

TO
THESE THREE
WHOSE PRESENCE MAKES
RETURNING HOME
THE BEST PART
OF
ANY JOURNEY

FOREWORD

FIFTEEN of the papers in this book have appeared in *The Scotsman*. "The Bannockburn Clock" appeared in *The Glasgow Herald*. The one on "Inchcolm" was written for the Scottish Motor Traction Company, who have not only made it possible to visit that most interesting island, but have done more than anyone else to open up the remoter parts of the Lothians and the Borders to the general public. The two papers on "East Lothian" and that on "Cramond and Barnbougle" are printed in their present form for the first time; the "Dream of Durisdeer" owes its origin to an article which appeared in *The Record* of the Church to which I belong.

In acknowledging the kind permission which has been given me to reprint them, I must thank Messrs Longmans, Green & Co. for allowing me to quote several verses from one of Andrew Lang's most heartsome poems, "Twilight on Tweed" (Collected Poems, 4 vols., 1923); also Miss Margaret Warrender for permission to use some verses from Lady John Scott's "Songs and Verses." I have also to acknowledge to Mr W. B. Yeats the use of two verses from "The Lake Isle of Innisfree" ("Poems," T. Fisher Unwin), and Mr Alfred Noyes for the quotation from "The Death of Chopin"; to Mr Lloyd Osbourne I am indebted for leave to quote from Stevenson's Poems.

Three photographs were most generously given to me by the late Dr Inglis Clark, and the others I owe to Major Clayton. Both of these friends are past masters in the art of the camera.

My only desire is, that others should take to the roads which I myself have so often travelled, and that they should find on them as much beauty and joy as I have found. A book with so many references to old-time history is bound to contain some mistakes. But even an erring Scot may serve as a guide to others who seek to know this land of home which he has learned to love.

T. R. B.

Note

In this new and revised edition some of the matter which seemed inappropriate to a book on The Borders and The Lothians has been left out.

Seven new chapters—V, VI, VII, VIII, X, XV and XVI, together with the latter part of Chapter XII, concerning Kirkbride and Wanlockhead, have been added.

All the new matter has appeared in *The Scotsman*.

T. R. B.

August 1937.

CONTENTS

CONTENTS

ILLUSTRATIONS

YARROW

Fair shines the sun, green grows, green grows the grass
   Upon thy braes, O Yarrow;
Yet minstrels who have ever sung thy praise
   Have linked thy name with sorrow.

The wild birds' cry, the far-off bleat of lambs,
   The hush of Yarrow flowing,
The old grey towers, the graves, the lone green graves,
   The rose in Yarrow growing.

Here no alarm, no clash of war, no strife,
   The lonely hills lie sleeping;
And yet, at summer noon, through all thy peace
   I hear a sound of weeping.

From out the silence of thy storied vale,
   O pensive, lonesome Yarrow,
There comes a sound from ancient far-off days
   Of keening and of sorrow.

Green grows the grass, fair shines, fair shines the sun
   Upon thy braes, O Yarrow,
But youth and love and cauld black death have linked
   Thy beauty with their sorrow.

As gleams of hope break through the glooms of life
   To brighten days of sorrow,
So sunbeams kiss with softening touch, and light
   The dowie dens of Yarrow.

Soft flows the stream, fair blooms, fair blooms the rose
   In thy quiet vale, O Yarrow,
But night and day, the lilt of long lost love
   Has mixed thy peace with sorrow.

I

RIVERS OF ROMANCE

ETTRICK, YARROW, AND TWEED

I

THE secret of living happily in a city is to be out of it as often as possible. Not that any true Scot could ever tire of the beauties of Edinburgh, but that there is something primitive in us all which makes us hunger for the open spaces of the earth and the glamour of roads and rivers and hills. In this grey motherland we look forward through a more or less drab and drippy winter to the coming of spring, and when the spring does come, with its snell winds and primrose banks, what warmth we do not find in it, we hope for when the summer days arrive. The summer has come and gone, scattering with a very niggard hand a warm day here and there to make the rainpools of yesterday gleam like jewels in the sun. And now autumn has got us in the grips of regret almost before we have realised that summer is dead.

That is why an Autumn Holiday is one of the most human of institutions, for it means that most people long for one more adventure into country places before they finally turn back the hands of the clock to the wintry hour. So, let us make one last glorious excursion, whether it be a long day's run in a car, two days on the homely old push-bike, or, best of all, a long week-end's walking tour. This time, let it be a pilgrimage to those unrivalled rivers of romance—Ettrick, Yarrow, and Tweed.

Selkirk is the natural beginning, or ending, for such a pilgrimage. For this little city of the Souters, above all the Border towns, sits with its high-set eyes looking into the sunset which casts a red mist over the waters of Ettrick, Yarrow, and Tweed, as they well-nigh wash its very doorsteps. There is nothing wild or impetuous in these Lowland rivers; nothing like the rush and tumble of the Garry and Tummel, which dash themselves in thunder over the rocks. The Highlander, like his rivers, is full of impulse and passion; but Ettrick, Yarrow, and Tweed, like the Border breed, are full of quiet restraint, silent with a strength which seldom lifts up its voice, and deeply steeped in the lore of centuries, from source to sea and bank to bank.

Two miles westward from Selkirk lies the meeting place of the waters of Ettrick and Yarrow, and three miles to the north-east from Selkirk this mingled stream falls into Tweed below Lindean. As we take the road up Ettrick it is a pleasant thing to see the long, low, stately House of Bowhill, standing in the sunshine among the woods, as though this latter-day home of the Buccleuchs had not hundreds of years of fighting Scotts behind it. Across the stream is Carterhaugh, the scene of the fairy ballad of "Tamlane," with Tamlane's

Well, and somewhere over by Bowhill, the site of Miles Cross where Janet waited for the fairy train. Here, too, is Oakwood Tower, where dwelt in the thirteenth century that famous wizard, Michael Scott, whose words had such super-natural power:

> The words that cleft Eildon hills in three,
> And bridled the Tweed with a curb of stone.

This fine old keep was built by Robert Scott in 1602, and afterwards became the property of Wat of Harden, who married the Flower of Yarrow. She was a siccar lass as well as a bonnie one, for when her larder was empty, she placed a pair of clean spurs in a covered dish on the dinner table, and Wat knew then to set his reiving lads galloping over the heather for some other beeftub better plenished than his own. The rooms must have been cribbed enough, for the tower measures only thirty-eight feet by twenty-three, and the walls are four and a half feet thick. But of the twenty or thirty peel-towers which once stood in the forest, and formed a refuge in time of war, none remains so well preserved to-day as Oakwood.

Continuing by Hutlerburn and Howford, where the river rushes through a rocky throat, we cross Ettrick Bridge and find ourselves in the pleasant village of Ettrickbridgend. This is the last village we shall see on our journey, for there is no other rural metropolis throughout the whole length of Ettrick and Yarrow. Just above the village the beauties of lower Ettrick begin, for the river runs for nearly a mile over a bed of jagged rock, and between steep wooded banks. Here is Newhouse

Linns, at the bottom of which is the " Loup," well
known to fishers, where many a fine fish has been
caught by fly or otherwise. It was here in the
autumn of 1831 that Sir Walter Scott paid his last
visit to the Forest, when the red tints were making
the banks of Ettrick glorious as they are doing to-
day. Shattered in body and mind, he looked down
on the Linns and the Loup, happy that he could

> Still feel the breeze down Ettrick break.

And here he would turn from the river and look
towards Kirkhope Tower, that little red, bare
defiant Border keep which holds the pass over to
Yarrow.

We now begin the real ride up Ettrick, and as it
is a long way to Potburn, at the head of the stream,
we shall sit down on the roadside for a little, by the
bridge that leads to Ettrick Shaws. It was while
sitting here trying to find an adjective to describe
the homely, comfortable beauty of Ettrick, that a
great Border shepherd came along and solved the
problem.

" A fine heartsome valley this."

" Ay, man; its a far *couthier* valley than Yarrow.
I've herded sheep up at Potburn, and never felt
dull in Ettrick a' my life. But there's a bareness
aboot Yarrow that makes ye feel fair melancholy.
But Yarrow has a great name—it was Wordsworth
gie'd it that—it's got the name, ye ken."

" It's the same wi' folk as places—there's a lot in
a name."

" Ay; either a guid yin or a bad yin."

There can be no doubt about it, *couthy* is the word for Ettrick, as *dowie* is the word for Yarrow. A kindly, agreeable, comfortable, pleasant vale is Ettrick, from Carterhaugh right up to Potburn, with no sense of melancholy. Yonder, across the river, at Singlie Farmhouse, James Hogg, when a lad, served with Mr Scott, and up the glen on the other side lies Dodhead, where " Jamie Telfer " lived in his tower at the foot of Black Rig. One day the English Captain of Bewcastle came and robbed Jamie of his kye. But Jamie followed him with his friends, and not only retook his cattle, but slew the English gentry, and, with true Scots relish for a fight, raided his enemy's home as well. At Gilmanscleuch it is the same—an old story of clash and battle between Scotts and Scotts.

Yonder, over the water, are the two farms which go by a strangely foreign-sounding name—Easter and Wester Deloraine. Old Scots history again, and more than one way of explaining this place-name. Some say that James II. gave his Queen the Forest of Ettrick as part of her dowry, these farms were named as the lands *de la reine*. Others find an explanation in the fact that Queen Mary's mother was Mary of *Lorraine*. But the name is probably far older than that, for there was an old Celtic Saint called *Orran*, and *dal-orran* means the " Place of Orran." A strange corroboration of this theory is the local pronunciation of the name, which holds in Ettrick to this day, for the people call it Del'orran. But who dare dogmatise? It is an interesting fact about Wester Deloraine that the Scottish poet, Henry Scott Riddell, minister of

Teviothead and author of "Scotland Yet," was for two years a shepherd here.

Stopping at Tushielaw Inn we keep thinking of Adam Scott of Tushielaw, that king of thieves whom James V. is said to have hanged in 1529 from a branch of an ash tree at the gate of his tower. But tradition can often be corrected by a search among the historical records; and Pitcairn, in his "Criminal Trials," records that Adam Scott was convicted in Edinburgh on 18th May 1530 "of are and part of the theftuously taking blackmail," and he adds one ominous word— "Beheaded."

The Rankleburn Glen opens on the south side of the river, opposite Tushielaw, and three miles up this glen is Buccleuch, the deep ravine where the traditional buck was slain. Kenneth III. (997-1005), the story goes, was hunting one day, and gave the Galloway keeper who slew the buck the right to call himself "John Scott of Buckscleuch." It is a far cry from the time of Kenneth and the ravine at Rankleburn to Bowhill House down the river, to-day the seat of the Duke of Buccleuch.

Two miles beyond Tushielaw stands the old tower and modern mansion-house of Thirlestane, the property of Lord Napier and Ettrick. Here the valley is wide and picturesque, with the long vale of Tima Water opening to the south.

At Ramsaycleuch and the post office of Ettrick we are in the very heart of Ettrick. It was at Ramsaycleuch that Sir Walter and the Ettrick Shepherd spent the first night of their acquaintance. Hogg was born in a cottage at Ettrickhall, half a mile up the road, and there is now a handsome monument near the site.

A little further on stands Ettrick Kirk, with the White Manse looking out from the trees across the valley. Here we are on holy ground, for Ettrick Kirk is the shrine of the whole vale. Standing with its square tower, and ivy-covered walls in a well-kept kirkyard, which is surrounded by great trees, here is a Scots country kirk that never disappoints us and is appropriate in all ways to the place. And among the green howes we find the resting places of old folks, both gentle and simple, who lived their span of years remote, and died as they would have wished, to be buried at last in Ettrick.

You will find the graves of four who have made Ettrick famous — Thomas Boston, minister of Ettrick, and author of " The Fourfold State ": James Hogg, the Ettrick Shepherd; Tibbie Shiel; and Will o' Phaup. For piety and pastoring there was none like Boston. Through a lifetime of sorrows he never spent a silent Sunday; and so thirled was his soul to Ettrick that, in his last painful illness, he preached through the open window of his manse to the hillfolk standing in the garden. James Hogg made Scotland sing with melody and the poetry of fairyland. Will o' Phaup, whose stone stands next the shepherd's, was the mighty athlete of the valley, and a shepherd for fifty-five years. How many strong men might envy his epitaph!

Here lyeth William Laidlaw, the far-famed
Will o' Phaup, who for feats of frolic, agility,
and strength had no equal in his day—age 84.

And Tibbie Shiel, that most famous of all inn-
keepers in Yarrow, whose grave you will find
against the kirkyard wall.

Isabella Shiel Richardson, ' Tibbie Shiel,'
d. 1878, age 96.

It is six miles further up to Potburn, a little farm
which stands alone, down in the hollow at the
head of the valley. On the way up you will pass
the farm of Phauphope standing by a little planta-
tion of fir trees on the other side of the river.
Here lived Will o' Phaup, whose daughter was the
mother of the Ettrick Shepherd. At this point is
Will's Loup, a great leap from rock to rock across
a pool which we measured with the eye, but had
not the courage to try, and yonder is a course of
a hundred yards over which he ran against time
every year, as he grew old, to see how much he had
lost in the year. Great Will o' Phaup—we take
off our hats to you, and wish more men had the
sense to keep so fit!

The road ceases to be luxurious for motors
beyond Broadgairhill, the next farm; but the true
traveller will trudge on till he comes to Potburn,
which, despite its lowly situation, is said to be the
highest farm in the Borders—1250 feet above sea
level. Just before coming to Potburn we get a
glimpse of the heartsome green hill road, that leads
the gangrel over the hills to Bodesbeck, on the

Moffat road. With another glance at Ettrick Pen, looking down on us from 2270 feet, we reluctantly turn our backs on Potburn and spin down the valley with our thoughts on Tushielaw Inn.

Having rested there, we take the road again at Crosslee, which leads from Ettrick into Yarrow, by the lonely farm of Berrybush. Having climbed the road to Berrybush it will, with some, be a swither whether they will take the easier road to the right which leads by Altrieve to the Gordon Arms, or the much rougher road to the left, which leads at last down a rather trying hill, to Tibbie Shiel's. Being a wandering man myself, I prefer the harder and the rougher road, for two reasons—you meet nobody on it, and there is always an extra spice in the adventure.

What memories cluster round Tibbie Shiel's famous little hostelrie—with its old box beds in the kitchen and its " Noctes Ambrosianæ "—Hogg, John Wilson, and the rest. One morning, when the bottles were empty, and Hogg was still thirsty, he implored Tibbie to " bring in the loch." On the day of this wonderful old woman's funeral men came from far and near to pay their respects to her memory. One man came over from Moffat, and not knowing the way, inquired of a stone-breaker, " Is it far to Tibbie's? " " Ay, man, it is that," replied the pawkie roadmaker, " Tibbie's deid."

Here, between the Loch o' the Lowes and St Mary's Loch, we pass down the road from Tibbie's to Hogg's monument, which stands where he wished it to be, " in some quiet spot fornent Tibbie's." The sculptor was Andrew Currie, who for long lived at Darnick Tower, near Melrose. What more appropriate line could adorn the Ettrick Shepherd's monument than the last line of his " Queen's Wake "?

He taught the wandering winds to sing.

RIVERS OF ROMANCE

II

PASSING along the road that skirts St Mary's Loch we are in the heart of Yarrow, and may well ask ourselves why Yarrow—this open valley, with the hills that are so soft in outline and so green to the top, should be so different from Ettrick and Tweed. For there is something pensive and haunting in the atmosphere of this storied stream. *Dowie* is the word for Yarrow. And yet it is very difficult to say why exactly Yarrow should give the traveller this catch at the heart. Perhaps it is that the old ballad lore and the local history are " drenched in the blood of love's tragedy "—stricken women who have won love at the great cost of dead brothers and fathers and friends; brave men who have ridden over hill and dale and fought on the green holms of Yarrow for the love of fair ladyes; little children crying for those who will never return; the tramp of king's cavalcades and the glitter of queen's retinues: all the ancient sadness and sacrifice of the dim centuries, which remind us of

> The old, unhappy far-off things,
> And battles long ago.

Set all this ageless drama of human love against the pastoral background of the serene hills, which are strangely reminiscent in their outlines, and you will perhaps understand why the beauty of Yarrow hurts even while it fascinates. A ballad meets you at every corner and in every grey old tower.

Crossing Meggat Water at the tiny hamlet of Cappercleuch, we are tempted to step a mile up the stream to Henderland, where stood the tower of Piers Cockburn of Henderland, another hardy Border thief, who, according to the tradition, was hanged on his own gate by James V. on that 1529 excursion which meant death also to Tushielaw. But it was not Piers or Perys Cockburn, but William Cockburn, to whom James V. gave such short shrift, and he was, almost beyond question, taken to Edinburgh along with Adam Scott of Tushielaw, where he was tried and executed. To-day at Henderland in a little wood, you will find the grave with its inscription—" Here lyis Perys of Cockburne and his wyfe Marjory." That moving ballad, " The Border Widow's Lament," tells the traditional story in most tragic language: how after Cockburn's death, his wife watched his body day and night alone, and then carried her dead lord on her own back and digged his grave with her own hand: —

> But think na ye my heart was sair,
> When I laid the moul' on his yellow hair;
> Oh, think na ye, my heart was wae,
> When I turned myself about to gae?

The Stuart Kings had a shooting box on Meggatland, and one August day in 1566 Queen Mary and Darnley rode down Megget Water and returned to Edinburgh by Traquair.

On the other side of the loch can be seen the farm of Bowerhope. Sandy Cunningham, a tenant there, was returning one summer Sunday from Ettrick Kirk and had just come in sight of his forest steading, sleeping in the sun by the shores of St Mary's Loch. The sermon had been on the joys of Paradise. But Sandy gazed on his home with hungry eyes and said, "Paradise here or Paradise there, gie me Bowerhope," and then, like a true Scot, he added under his breath, "at a raisonable rent!"

But the spot of holiest memories on St Mary's Loch, and, indeed, in all Yarrow, is up on the hillside to the left, where, after some little search, you will find all that remains of the site of St Mary's Kirk, a grey wall enclosing some graves, and a rail-encircled tomb in which grow great yews and box shrubs. Mention was first made of St Mary's in Yarrow in 1275, when Bagimund came from Rome to Scotland to gather benefices for the Crusades. An old, old story now! but to stand here in the silence and loneliness among the graves of six centuries is to view St Mary's at its sad and dowie best. Dream a little longer, and with Hamilton of Bangour, you begin to see this same St Mary's bowered in trees, and the monks' orchards all round where

Fair hangs the apple frae the rock.

Monks and knight-errants, fair ladies and plain hill folks, Kings and Queens and reiving Border lords, lovers in the gloaming, and hardy cattle-lifters—they all met here, and mingled history with poetry, and tradition with ballad lore, until in 1557 we see St Mary's Kirk ablaze, when the Cranstouns and Buccleuchs were clashing swords in a deadly feud, after burning the holy place. Now

> All is loneliness;
> And silence aids, tho' the steep hills
> Send to the lake a thousand rills:
> In summertime so soft they weep,
> The sound but lulls the ear asleep:
> Your horse's hoof-tread sounds too rude
> So stilly is the solitude.

A little further on, up the burn on the left, stands Dryhope Tower, the birthplace of Mary Scott, that Flower of Yarrow who married Walter Scott of Harden.

> Then gaze on Dryhope's ruined tower.
> And think on Yarrow's faded flower.

Douglas Burn is the next stream, and here indeed we touch storied ballad ground; for about a mile and a half up the stream stands Blackhouse Tower, the scene of the Douglas tragedy. Lord William comes to Blackhouse, and carries off Lady Margaret. He springs to the saddle, and pounds up the old hill road to Tweed with his beloved sitting before him. The mother discovers the runaways. She calls upon her husband and her seven sons to be after them. They overtake the lovers in the glen. Lord William dismounts and bids Lady Margaret stand aside, while he draws his sword. One after another, he slays the seven brothers, and wounds the father, and then rides on. But his own blood runs red in the stream where they stop to bathe his wounds.

> Lord William was dead lang e'er midnight;
> Lady Margaret lang ere day.

> Lord William was buried in St. Mary's kirk,
>   Lady Margaret in Mary's quire;
> Out of the lady's grave grew a bonny red rose,
>   And out o' the knight's a brier.

There you have the dowie spirit of Yarrow. Love and loss; battle and wounds; death and the old kirkyard among the hills.

Up this very glen James Hogg herded sheep. Up here Jock Scott first recited " Tam o' Shanter " to him, and told him about the Ayrshire ploughman, Robert Burns. Hogg bristled at the mention of the ploughman. " I could tell mair stories and sing mair songs than ever ploughman in the world." And so he did. Here, Willie Laidlaw, Sir Walter's amanuensis, was born—he who wrote " Lucy's Flittin'." All the love and lore of Yarrow seems to ride down Douglas Burn.

The name of Hogg brings us to the Gordon Arms Inn, where Scott said good-bye to the Ettrick Shepherd for the last time in 1830—" Sir Walter leaning heavily on Hogg's arm and walking very feebly." Exactly twenty-nine years before, Hogg had met Scott for the first time at his mother's cottage at Ettrickhall. He worshipped Sir Walter; but he was such a simple-minded man that, when Sir Walter arranged a meeting between Hogg and the Duke of York at Richmond Park with a view to a pension for the Shepherd Poet, Hogg declined because that day, July 18, was St Boswell's Fair, and he had to be there! Away across the valley yonder at Altrieve Lake, Hogg lived for years in a new house which the Duke of Buccleuch gifted to him, and the only stipulation which the shepherd made was that " a' the reek should come oot at ae lum," so that when he had a house full of visitors there would be no sign that any but the goodwife was at home! Up there too, at Mount Benger Farm, Hogg lived and lost money grandly, because he liked poetry and friends and fairies better than farming. It was above Mount Benger, on the Traquair road, that Wordsworth first saw Yarrow, and we must never forget that it was Hogg who guided Wordsworth during his Yarrow tour: —

> Where first descending from the moorlands,
> I saw the stream of Yarrow glide
> Along a bare and open valley,
> The Ettrick Shepherd was my guide.

The lower reaches of Yarrow begin at the Gordon Arms, and, travelling back towards Selkirk down this storied vale we keep picking up ballad and tradition all the way. Near Yarrow Kirk, on the farm of Whitehope, we come to the Dowie Dens, where the famous battle was fought. Yon two standing stones could tell the tale that no man for certain knows to-day, if only they could speak— but one of them at least has an old inscription on it—"Hic memoriæ et . . . hic jacent in tumulo duo filii liberali." Whatever the story of these two brothers be, or the story of the song, or the cause of the duel, here at least in this hollow we have the traditional site of the tragedy, and to the end of time that quiet "houm" in Yarrow will remain the Dowie Dens.

In Yarrow Kirkyard, close by, you will find the grave of John Rutherford, the maternal great-grandfather of Sir Walter Scott. In the old kirk, while the dogs sat with their masters, the shepherds, it was the habit to pronounce the benediction before the congregation arose, as the rising of the worshippers was the signal for a babel of yelping when the long service was over. This was called "the cheating o' the dowgs." The newly restored kirk is a gem of beauty, although the old plain kirks fit the glens of Scotland better than the new.

The scenery becomes more beautiful with wood-lands as we descend the valley. Hangingshaw, the chief seat in the old days of the famous outlaw Murray, has always been renowned for its great trees. Here the old road over Minchmoor descends on Yarrow near Broadmeadows. High up on that road Sir Walter said good-bye to Mungo Park, the African traveller, who was born at Foulshiels. Over that road the great Montrose fled with the remnant of his troops after his one and only de-feat at Philiphaugh. Across Yarrow stands stately

B

Newark Tower, so called to contrast it from a very ancient tower called Auldwark, which stood close by. And here is Philiphaugh House, below which the battle of 1645 took place. After this defeat there was nothing left for the great Marquis but to make over Minchmoor and meet the misfortunes which led to his ultimate fate in the Capital—a noble head stuck on a pike in the High Street for all and sundry to gaze at. So Yarrow, which begins at St Mary's with the hanging of Cockburn of Henderland, and the Douglas Tragedy of nine dead men at Blackhouse, travels all its way past duel grounds and battlefields and falls into Ettrick with the greatest battle of all at Philiphaugh, a water of lost loves and a river of song, but always a stream with a sough of sorrow in it.

To those who would go home by Abbotsford and Galashiels, the road crosses the water into Selkirk, and then keeps down the south side of the river to Lindean. But for us perfection lies up Tweed to Peebles. He is a poor Scot indeed whose mind is not stored with many memories of Tweed—that fairest of all Scots rivers, which rises away up at Tweed's Well and falls into the sea at Berwick. To know the Tweed from its cradle among the Border hills to its mouth, where in these autumn days the fishermen will be landing their last catch of salmon for the season under the old sea wall—that is to take with you about the world an unseen library of poetry and romance and the memory of beauty, which in old age will be a blessed consolation. For no river in Scotland can compare with that one hundred and three miles for beauty, ballad lore, and ancient legendry. We are thankful, on this golden autumn day, to travel up these fifteen or sixteen miles, which, even on Tweedside, are hard to beat. The very names of the places we pass make music in the ear— Yair, Fairnilee, Holylee, Ashiestiel, Elibank, and Traquair.

In that old turret of Fairnilee, Alison Rutherford (who became Mrs Cockburn), wrote "The Flowers of the Forest." Yonder across the river, dreaming among the trees, is the old house of Yair, where the Pringles made history, and carved long ago this epitaph in a chapel of Melrose Abbey: "Here lies the race of the House of Zair." On a blue-white day of spring, or a warm day of midsummer, or a still autumn day, when the world is all russet and gold, the Tweed at Yair is as fair as fair can be. Beyond Caddonfoot the bridge leads you over to the old south-side road up Tweed—Sir Walter's road, be it ever remembered—but the new road is the one which all the world follows now. Yonder, beyond the new house of Peel, stands Ashiestiel, leased by Sir Walter Scott in 1804 from his cousin General Russell. He lived in his romantic house for eight years, and here he wrote "The Lay of the Last Minstrel," "Marmion," "The Lady of the Lake," and the first chapter of "Waverley." Had he been able to buy Ashiestiel, Clarty Hole would never have become Abbotsford. The house is much changed now, but old Ashiesteil will for ever be Scott's true Border setting.

A mile past Thornilee, on the wooded heights

across the river, stands Elibank—the old tower in ruins on the hill above, the new house in the woods below. This was a favourite Sunday walk of Scott's, when doubtless he often recalled his ancestry, for here it was that young Scott of Harden preferred Muckle-Mouthed Meg to the gallows.

No man of sensibility could pass through Inner-leithen without a desire to look at the old House of Traquair on the other side of the river. Like many another, such as Dunvegan Castle in Skye, it is said to be the oldest inhabited house in Scotland. But what matter? It is very old, very quaint, and very Scottish—standing in its green seclusion. We view it through the ancient gates between pillars with the Bradwardine Bears atop—the model of Scott's gateway of Tully Veolan in "Waverley." The old Earls of Traquair, red hot Jacobite Stuarts every one of them, have left a pathetic legacy in the family decree, that these great gates are never to be opened until a Stuart King rides down the wide grass pleasaunce to the door. Many a Scots King, from Malcolm III., passed the doorsteps of Traquair. The first Earl was Lord High Treasurer of Scotland, and King's Commissioner to the Kirk, but before all was done he begged on the streets of Edinburgh. He is mentioned in the ballad of "Christie's Will."

Traquair has ridden up Chapel Hope,
And sae has he down by the Grey Mare's Tail;
He never stinted the light gallop,
Until he speer'd for Christie's Will.

THE CLOSED GATES OF TRAQUAIR

He was something of a wag, for in order to gain
a lawsuit on one occasion, he had the Lord Presi-
dent of the Court of Session kidnapped while he
was riding on Leith sands.   After the decision, the
poor judge was set down again on the very spot
where he had been lifted.

> Traquair has written a private letter,
> And he has sealed it wi' his seal,
> Ye may let the auld brock out o' the pock;
> My land's my ain, and a's gane weel!

The Eighth and last Earl was a true friend of the
rich and a willing helper of the poor.   He died in
1861, and his sister, the Lady Louisa, followed him
fourteen years later.

In Traquair Kirkyard we sit and sing to ourselves
another tune of romance—John Campbell Shairp's
" Bush aboon Traquair," which was founded on
an older poem, and is perhaps the finest example
we have of a modern border ballad.

> Will ye gang wi' me and fare
> To the bush aboon Traquair?
> Ow're the High Minchmuir we'll up and awa,
> This bonny simmer noon,
> While the sun shines fair aboon,
> And the licht sklents saftly doun on holm an' ha'.

> And what would ye do there
> At the bush aboon Traquair?
> A lang dreigh road, ye had better let it be:
> Save some auld skrunts o' birk
> I' the hillside lirk,
> There's nocht i' the warld for man to see.

The scrunts of birk, the Quair burn, the kirk-yard, and the lang dreich road are all here yet. Yonder up the Quair burn is the road to Glen House—Lord Glenconner's seat—where in the old forest steading (mentioned in history as far back as 1216) there lived long ago that old Covenanter, Veitch of Glen. Here, at a still later date, was born Captain Porteous of the City Guard, who was hanged on a dyer's pole in the Grassmarket by the Porteous Mob in 1736. Up there on the left is the road over Minchmoor—the "lang dreich road" which the lover took from Yarrow to keep his tryst at the Bush of Traquair; but to him the road would be short. Here, in the old kirkyard, generations of such lovers lie, well-happed beneath the green howes; and you may even pull a bit of birk on the hillside yet to remind you that, although everything dies and passes in this old world, true love is as fresh and new to-day as it ever was.

With that we make for Peebles, the end and the beginning of many a happy journeying through the border land. An old-farrant place, with a bagful of history all its own—did not King James I. write "Peblis to the Play"? And through its streets has not the clash and clang of Border Raiding and Romance kept this ancient Burgh on Tweed in life and love from one century to another? But that story would take a long time in the telling. Our pilgrimage is over. So, with a last look at Tweed in the darkening, we hear some one singing the old lilt which will mingle with our dreams this very night under the harvest moon.

They were blest beyond compare,
When they held their trysting there,
Amang thae greenest hills shone on by the sun;
And then they wan a rest,
The lownest and the best,
I' Traquair Kirkyard when a' was dune.

III

THE HOMELY VALE

HE was indeed a Scots visionary who once spoke this message of comfort to a stricken soul: " Heaven never looks half so beautiful as when the trees have been stripped of all their leaves." To the Nature lover the winter landscape is just as beautiful in its own way as the summer landscape. Sometimes it is far more beautiful in its low colour tones. One appreciates the character of a tree better when its trunk is bare, its branches clean-stripped, and the delicate tracery of its myriad twigs stands out against the liquid skies of a sunny morning in December or January.

How full of sensitive purples, amethysts, blues, and greys are the mists that hang over the hollows of a ploughed field! Or look along the unpruned hawthorn hedges on a quiet winter forenoon, when not a sound breaks the holy calm, and you will see the same atmosphere of purples and blues like fairy whiffs of smoke where the hedgerows line each side of the clarty road. The blue-green strips of the Swedish turnips and the verdant green of the Whites make splashes of brilliance side by side on the low-toned wintry fields. The tawny colour of the hills, and the long white grasses that wave on Pentland or Lammermoor in the dead months of the year, always recall the words of that auld-farrant gentlewoman, Lady John Scott, "Heaven won't seem heaven if I don't see those benty fields and tufts of rushes there!" For the wind of the Lammermoors was the very breath of her soul.

But there is a veritable painter's palette of winter beauty which I never can pass without thinking how prodigally Nature lavishes her best work on the humblest of subjects. It is a poor little bit of boggy moorland beyond Leadburn. Most people associate Leadburn with weary waits at a junction, bleak moors, and snell, biting winds. Certainly one would not choose to be caught here in an on-ding of rain, or hail, or snow; for the road at its highest point is nine hundred and thirty-one feet, and the world about Leadburn has no bield. But how few of those who in motor cars race down Eddleston Water have time, or the eyes, to see the beauty of this wind-swept scrap of water-logged moorland, or to look back and gaze on the splendid panorama of the Pentland range stretched from end to end! On this perfect January morning the blazing sun is melting the white rime on road and moorland, except where it lies in the shadow of bank or hummock. This bog is not for anyone with slippered feet. But as I stand in the centre and look under the rim of the hat towards the low sun, this little patch of moor marsh is like a crumpled carpet of greens and browns and blacks, with the Moorfoots and the hills of Tweed rolling away in long misty billows until they are lost in the haze. A hare rises from a hummock,

> And with her feet, she from the plashy earth
> Raises a mist that, glittering in the sun,
> Runs with her all the way, wherever she doth run.

All the ochres and umbers, burnt siennas, and Vandyke browns of Nature's palette are here this wintry morning. The little dubs and pools flash in the sunshine, and when the day is done reflect the crimson and gold of the glowing west. Come again in summer and you will see these peat haggs glorified with purple heather. Wild flowers star the moss with heliotrope and yellow, and the white cotton grass waves its snowy flags in the sun-kissed wind. Here is a poor little moss between the road and the railway, of no use to man or beast, ringed about with barbs as a place of danger, but on this sunny morning not all the jewels on earth can equal it for beauty.

Leaving the windy heights of Leadburn, a turn past Craigburn on the left, with its scrunts of trees and its milestone, brings us face to face with Eddleston Valley. Even a tar-sprayed road—that abomination of trampers and horsemen—may have its winter beauty. For the sun has now melted the frost on its smooth surface, and the long, straight, dazzling road looks like a river of molten silver flowing between the benty moors. Now we reach the bridge beneath which flows the modest stream of Eddleston Water, and on our right runs an ancient grass-grown road. As we

get further down the valley, the growing volume
of the stream reminds us that, in the language of
the Borders, a "water" is larger than a burn,
and yet not quite large enough to be a river.
The scenery of this homely vale is quiet, but it is
the early vale of dream to me, because to a burgher
of Auld Reekie it is the nearest outgait to the
Border Country. Here, indeed, is our pilgrim's
path to Scotland's Rivers of Romance. From the
very name of its highest homesteads a January
traveller draws honied hopes of spring. Earlyvale,
Earlypier, Earlyburn—did ever a place-namer make
a better show of poetry in a plain-featured valley?

But Eddleston Water has its old-world story as
well as its human interests to-day, for all these
lands were ancient church lands belonging to the
See of Glasgow. The earliest British name of the
district was Peniacob or Penteiacob. This name
appears in the inquest of Prince David as early as
1116. Within fifty years this British name was
changed to the Norman name of Gillemorestun,
after a settler called Gillemor, and before twenty
years had passed (1189) the manor of Gillemorestun was granted to an Anglo-Saxon called Edulf,
the son of Utred, from whom it took the name
of Edulfstoun, by which it is still known. But
enough of old-time records: let us rather hear
the more human tales of the lands and lairds and
common folks of this pleasant vale of Eddleston.

Most people have forgotten all about the Earl
who gave his name to the place of Portmore, for
his title has been exinct for nearly ninety years.
But many a passer-by remembers that the place

was once the home of Forbes Mackenzie. And yet
I would rather think of Portmore in connection with
his youngest brother, who left this quiet valley and
became a famous Bishop in South Africa. There
he met a soul that was sib to his own—David
Livingstone—and set a standard of Christian conduct
which is for ever memorialised in these words:
" If there was any Christian deed to be done, any
work of mercy to be performed, either for the
bodies or souls of men, then Mackenzie's whole
heart was engaged. To go about doing good was
the only employment which he thoroughly and
unreservedly loved."

A sleepy place is Eddleston village on this January
day, with winter sunshine sklenting through the
trees, and the old kirk standing on the hill. The
only sounds to be heard are the lowing of cattle,
the chirrup of partridges down by the water, the
crowing of a cock, the rumble of cartwheels in
the distance, and the ring of the anvil in the
smiddy with its two curious horse-shoe windows.
The little school has a quaint outside bell. The
kirkyard gate is fastened by a bit of string. The
kirk itself is a combination of things old and
new, with a sundial high up on the corner of the
wall, old carved stones built into the belfry gable,
and by the vestry door, grey memorials with the
well-known names of Murray, Whyte Melville, and
Wolfe on them, and a tale in tombs of four
Robertsons who ministered here for one hundred
and seventy-five years. A very old Murray stone
bears this downright confession of faith—*Deum
timeo*—I fear God.

But across the valley yonder there lived long ago a Murray who feared no man. Blackbarony, now an hotel, was the seat of the Elibank Murrays, and the sight of this old white Scots house, which is built after the manner of a French château, reminds us of Sir Gideon Murray, who founded this branch of the ancient house of Blackbarony. Hs was a fine example of Scots thrift and summary justice.

The thrift on one occasion showed itself in yon wide grass avenue which runs up to the mansion. There are only three such grand grass approaches in Peebleshire—at Traquair, at Dawyck, and here at Blackbarony. Sir Gideon, when entertaining distinguished guests, used to post his retainers in livery at the foot of the trees in this long avenue, with an instruction that the servants were to run round the back of the trees whenever the guests had passed and take their posts behind the trees higher up. This gave a stranger the impression that the Darnhall retainers were countless in number.

His summary justice had also a smack of self-interest, for it was this same long-headed freebooter and master of bluff who gave William Scott of Harden—Sir Walter's ancestor—the cheery choice of being hanged or of marrying Sir Gideon's rather plain-faced daughter, who was nicknamed " Muckle Mouthed Meg." Little wonder that the pawkie Scot touches his hat to Darnhall as he travels down Eddleston Water and winks quietly at old Elibank Tower as he journeys down Tweed.

Still further down this homely vale stands the red house of Cringletie—a name with a fine Scots bite in it. It is the home of the Wolfe-Murrays, one of whom served under General Wolfe at Quebec in 1750, and thereafter adopted the name of that great soldier. Another was raised to the Bench as Lord Cringletie. His wife was Isabella Strange, a grand-daughter of Sir Robert Strange the famous engraver, who engraved the bank notes used in Prince Charlie's army. Before being raised to the Bench, Lord Cringletie was one of the counsel for the prosecution in the famous Deacon Brodie case. I like to look at the portrait of the late James Wolfe-Murray, a spare, white-bearded, old man, dressed in a kilt, and seated on his white Russian shooting pony, called "Moscow," with a feather in his hat and his gun cocked ready for a shot. He was a gey sportsman, and used to keep a silver flute and a pea-rifle in his bedroom. Early in the morning he would quietly open the window and play "Rousseau's Dream" or "Robin Adair" in dulcet tones, until the rabbits came out to listen. Then the silver flute was silent, the pea-rifle spoke, and Master Bunny lay low for ever. A keeper once said of this adventurous sportsman, "Maister Wolfe-Murray wad shoot his gran-mither if she war risin' afore him!"

Few people passing down Eddleston Water give any thought to the little cottage called Redscaurhead on the roadside just below Cringletie Bridge. But it was here that George Meikle Kemp came on the 14th day of June 1809 from his father's house at Moorfoot. He was only fifteen years of age, and he was apprenticed to Andrew Noble, who was then the carpenter at Redscaurhead. In his second year of apprenticeship, young Kemp walked over to Roslin to feast his eyes on the 'Prentice Pillar and all the other restless miracles of the carver's craft in the chapel. One June day in 1813 he left Eddleston Water for new employment at Galashiels, meaning to trudge the seventeen miles on foot with his tools on his shoulder. But when near old Elibank Tower he got a lift in a lumbering chaise from a gentleman who was lame. When they reached Galashiels Kemp got out with his tools, thanked his benefactor for his kindness, and asked a bystander who the gentleman was. To his astonishment, he found that he had been befriended by Walter Scott—the Shirra. Little did Scott think that the youth who thanked him so modestly for the ride was yet to design the magnificent Scott Monument which stands in Princes Street to-day. Years after that ride, when Kemp was making a sketch of a part of Melrose Abbey, Scott came into the Abbey grounds with a company of friends. He began immediately to watch the artist at work, without knowing who he was. But Kemp knew the great Romancer by sight, and was just waiting to hear him speak when suddenly Maida, the beloved staghound, had to be restrained in some frolic, and Scott hastened away to call the dog to heel. Scott and Kemp never met again, but the architect never ceased to regret his lost opportunity.

We began this January day with thoughts of winter beauty; now the sun is setting as we trudge into Peebles. Crossing Tweed Bridge, which road should a lover take but the footpath up the river opposite Neidpath? Here, in the solemn hush of twilight, listening to the swirl of the water beneath the trees, the old castle rises like a ghost of romance above the green terraces of the hanging gardens where lords and ladies wandered long ago. A touch of sunset tips the tree-tops, but Tweed whispers its secret in the gloom below. For this is the endless joy of Eddleston Water, that it lures us like a lover who is always glad to take the shortest road to the river of his heart—Tweed.

IV

THE DIARY OF A TWEEDSIDE LAIRD

A HUNDRED YEARS AGO

It is a little old passbook with money columns and marled boards, and the charm of it to an imaginative Scot who loves the ancient lore of his land is, that it gives no clue to the name of the Border laird who wrote it, nor does it name the actual place where he dwelt. But, at least, it makes clear that the house itself was near Innerleithen; that Peebles was the nearest town; and that our own city at that date was the romantic Edinburgh of Scott and Jeffrey, Christopher North and De Quincey, Carlyle and Chalmers. We have travelled so far in custom and knowledge since then that it is a heartsome thing to put on our horn spectacles and take the antiquary's glance into the past life of this Tweedside laird—and, to those who are old enough, it will be a pleasant puzzle to find out who the laird was, and where his mansion stood.

To begin with, he was a well-off man, according to the standards of the Georgian days in which he lived. This passbook gives us his expenses for one summer only, from 3rd June to 14th October 1830, and his expenditure, including a trip to London, amounted to £545. At the end of the book we find a note of his income from 3rd June to 26th July, and it is from three sources—from a certain Mr Richardson and a certain Mr Melville, W.S., the first of whom seems to have been his " doer "; from Messrs Coutts, bankers in London; and from local rents and cut timber sold to a local carpenter. These two months alone yielded him an income of £810. A truly canny laird, as other items will show.

He kept a coach and a stable boy, a gardener and an apprentice, indoor servants, and an orra-man, and when he travelled he took with him Robert Scott, as his body servant, to valet him. He farmed his own land, and paid £75, 10s. 6d. in wages for the half-year to his farm servants. To Frank Heath, who looked after the stallion, he paid sometimes £8, and sometimes £5, and when he ordered candles from Bogie the tallow-chandler at Selkirk he bought them in £5 parcels. So we can with safety conclude that the laird's house stood in its own well-timbered grounds, with a farm near Innerleithen, that the gardens were considerable, that he bred horses, felled his own trees, and in winter lit his mansion with a respectable blaze of soft candlelight. Moreover, he was, like some other lairds, loath to give in to new ways; for in this very year, 1830, new roads were being made in many parts of Scotland, and the following entry might quite well point to the laird defying the march of progress: " Paid to John Hope for stopping the new road at Innerleithen, £2 "— unless, indeed, the word ' stopping ' bears some other meaning than hindering.

In those days when a Tweedside man travelled to London, he had to choose between the stage-coach and the steam vessel. So when our Laird travelled south, he went by sea and returned by post-chaise. It was a far cry from St Ronan's Well to Piccadilly, but all the gaiety of Vauxhall never seemed to displace the love which this careful Scot kept in his heart for the Vale of Tweed. Let us wander through his accompt-book, and the story will unfold itself.

The wages question was easily solved—for, John Nicholson the gardener got only £20 a year, with £4 for coals; the under gardener got £6, 10s.; and the orraman, when he was required, got 8s. a week. The housemaids—how many there were we do not know—cost the laird altogether £42 a year. A cart of coals cost 8s. 6d. His wine cost him £17, 14s. 1d., for one lot, from Bell & Rannie, of Leith; he got his groceries from Thorburn, of Leith; and there is another item of £7, 10s. 1d. to Walter Thorburn, merchant, at Peebles. The henwife, Margaret Burnet, was paid £3, and even his payments to " the Boy La Grieve for tapes, needles, and pins " are put down at 2s. But he does not grudge paying one Maclashan 7s. 6d. for drawing a coat-of-arms. Where are these arms to-day? And what name did they uphold? Who was the laird himself?

He was a Roman Catholic Laird on Tweedside, with Jacobite leanings. For, on 21st June, he paid to one Boyd " for the piper's dress of tartan " the sum of £2, 8s. 2d.; the next month we find him paying 5s. for four tickets for the pipers' ball at Innerleithen; again, in the same month, he pays 10s. to a man called Cameron for piping; and, last of all, in the same month of July, this Laird, who

kept his own piper and attended the pipers' ball, paid
2s. 6d. for " a pamphlet by Mr Nuxenbeth on
Defence of the Catholic Church."

Some of the items make delicious reading. He
seems to have been continually paying threepence
for the Peebles toll, and sometimes " for the mule "
—surely an unusual animal for a laird. But the
laird's mule must have been well known from
Peebles to Selkirk, from Leithen waters to Traquair
—for when the stable boy was sent " to Galashiels
with the mule " it cost one shilling. Two counter-
pane bed curtains cost him five pounds eight and
a penny and his newspaper sixpence halfpenny—and
he paid for his castor oil six and six a bottle, a deadly
dear dram. When he wrote to London an ordinary
letter cost one and threepence. Moreover, he was
a member of the St. Ronan's Border Club, which
entailed an annual subscription of ten shillings—so
one could be a club member for a whole year in those
blessed days for about the price of a bottle of castor
oil! But a Scotsman's spending has always shown
some originality in the matter of proportion, for
while the laird did not grudge to pay nine pounds
three shillings for meal for the dogs in his kennels,
he calmly puts down sixpence for charity.

Other items of purchase interest us greatly in these
present days of high prices. A hundred years ago
you could get a cart of coals for eight and six. He
slumps, without any conscience, " different articles
bought for the house " with a round entry of ten
pounds—and then he details the price of a lead
pencil, a turnpike toll, or a penny bun. Sugar then
cost tenpence a pound. But his sundries range from

ten pounds to twopence—a trick which is as old as
human nature, and may point to a quick-eyed wife
at home.

But it is when he leaves home that he becomes
most interesting. He travels to Edinburgh by the
Peebles coach, taking his man-servant with him,
which cost him thirteen and six for the two seats.
These two—the laird and the serving-man—seem
always to have gone to entertainments together, as
there are always two tickets purchased. Some simple
souls might infer that the laird was a widower, for
he never mentions his wife. But there are many
much married men who never mention their wives.
I rather think that our laird was not only a married
man, but that he had three daughters; for, although
he says nothing about his family, and gives no
indication of there being a boy, yet, after enjoying
his little flings in town with his serving-man, he
makes up for it by bringing home on one occasion a
fine shawl and three muslin dresses for girls. We
have only to compare the three muslin dresses with
the four tickets bought for the pipers' ball at Innerleithen to be almost certain that on that gay occasion
the laird took his three girls to the ball, for the
laird's lady, it is to be presumed, would not care
to go, and he himself was the last man to buy five
tickets if four were only to be used.

In Edinburgh he always stayed at Simpson's
Hotel. It was evidently not a cheap place, for he
paid five pounds ten shillings for a four-days' stay.
His tips varied from three shillings to one shilling,
except on one occasion when he gave ten. On his
arrival in town he writes home, which costs him

sevenpence. But it is when he goes shopping in
Auld Reekie that the laird shines, for he buys a
lead pencil at sixpence, a new neckcloth (cotton) at
one and six, a shaving brush, some shaving soap,
and a shaving box at two shillings each. Gaining
courage, he begins to plunge, for the same day he
buys a muslin gown at a pound and a silk hat for
himself at thirteen shillings—prices which make a
man with a family of daughters to-day groan with
envy. He next goes to the hairdresser and gets
himself done up for three shillings, has his razors
sharpened for another shilling, and thus prepares
himself for a trip to London.

It is all detailed. The coach from Edinburgh
down to the landing-stage at Newhaven cost him
four and six, the tolls one shilling, and the driver
one and six—seven shillings to go a mile or two.
There he hails a porter and a row-boat, gets his
luggage aboard, and is rowed out to the steam vessel,
with Robert Scott, his servant, sitting in the stern
sheets. The very first item on board is a modest
dram—a pint of port wine for himself at half a
crown, and a bottle of porter at a shilling for his
man. After master and servant are thus regaled on
the heaving vessel, the tickets are taken out—five
pounds cabin for the laird and two pounds twelve
and six steerage for the servant. There was, however,
no drinking on the voyage. Indeed, whisky is never
mentioned in the diary. The only other item of that
kind on the voyage to London was another pint of
sherry wine for the laird and a second bottle of
porter for the serving-man. The steward got half
a crown and the boots on board one shilling.

The voyage did not take long, for they left New-haven early on August 8th, and reached London the next evening or early on the morning of the 10th. This time-table tallies exactly with that given in one of the original Edinburgh almanacks for 1839 which lies before me—that is, nine years later—where the note under the London steamers is as follows: "The passage is frequently performed within forty hours, and the average passage is about forty-four hours."

On reaching London, they drove in the stage-coach from Blackwall to Leadenhall; there they hired a private coach and drove straight to Berkeley Street, where a sufficiently stylish lodging was engaged by the laird. Contrast this aristocratic address in Mayfair with his first purchase—$\frac{1}{2}$ lb. of sugar for 5d., and two rolls of bread for 2d.

They arrived in London on 10th August and left for home on 29th September; and during these seven weeks the laird spent £102, 3s. 5d., and the details are intensely interesting. The first day he buys a pair of three-and-sixpenny gloves, and then he goes on from one extravagance to another. What a jolly, innocent, frugal time he had! If we could only see his letters home, they would remind us of John Galt's laird Pringle, in "The Ayrshire Legatees" when he spent his immortal holiday in London.

I can only very briefly indicate some of the laird's ploys in town. He evidently had to find his own victuals, even in Berkeley Street—or rather he must have preferred to do so—for we find him buying his own tea (at 6s. the pound) as well as his own sugar; muffins and fresh butter; butter milk; cephalic snuff;

a corkscrew; another lead pencil; twenty-five quill pens; two buns; two tartlets; a French spelling book; and a box of pins at sixpence. Everything is bravely noted—even remorselessly entered up in this pass-book, like a man who has to give an account of his own soul every time he goes home.

But the same simple, pleasure-loving Scots laird who went to an equestrian entertainment at Inner-leithen and the pipers' ball, seeks out the musical entertainments in London and pays his shillings and sixpences with a royal extravagance. He is the strict Catholic all through, and is a regular attendant at the Spanish Chapel, where his seat usually costs him one and sixpence. A shilling is sometimes given to a street musician. The Prague minstrels and the chin musical performer cost him two shillings each— there is evidence of a companion here. He pays for seeing through a large microscope, and goes twice over (like a true Scot) to see statues of Tam o' Shanter and Souter Johnny in Bond Street. He pays to see the Thames tunnel, and more than once visits the "Colliseum." So it is quite evident that he enjoys himself in a strictly one-and-sixpenny way.

He has even his little flutter at gambling, and is honest enough to note down all his losses at the cartes! They range from thirteen shillings to one shilling. But what is that, when we find over the page that he paid ten shillings to have his corns cut, and squandered one pound eighteen shillings on a ruby pen for himself? A letter which he sends to Selkirk costs him three shillings and threepence. He goes to dioramas at Regent's Park. He visits Astley's circus and Covent Garden. He goes to

Vauxhall Gardens (four tickets) and to a cosmorama (six tickets)—but we are left in complete, or rather discreet, ignorance of his three companions at Vauxhall, and we will never know who were his five companions at the cosmorama. The diary is strictly financial—but even lairds are human. A flying visit to Tunbridge Wells broke the monotony; here he lost only one shilling at the card table. Then he returns to London and pays his bills: To Tautz, the tailor, fifteen pounds; for his lodgings in London, thirteen pounds thirteen and six (surely cheap for Berkeley Street!); for Robert Scott's board, four pounds nine shillings; and for his own posting to Edinburgh, seven pounds.

But before leaving London he bought several presents—all for ladies. One blue moreen travelling bag for four shillings, and a five-guinea shawl; one print muslin gown at thirty shillings; another ditto of buff colour at fifteen shillings; and a third ditto of pink colour at thirteen shillings. Surely here, at last, we have certain proof of the laird's never-mentioned wife at home and his three daughters. This dressmaker's bill, in this present year of grace, ought to be enshrined in our City Museum.

It was still October when he reached home, and on those Indian summer days on Tweedside I can see the laird's lady and her three girls sunning themselves one afternoon among the gillyflowers and late roses—the lady with her fine London shawl on her shoulders, the girls in their white and buff and pink high-wasted muslin gowns; while the laird himself, in his knee-breeches and stiff cotton stock, relates the wonders of Astley's circus and the diorama to his listening women folk, but never mentions Vauxhall or the cartes!

The last items in the book are his expenses between Edinburgh and Peebles. This music-loving Scots laird, who gave a boy a sixpence on a London street for playing a musical instrument, and then entered the item solemnly in his book, no sooner sets foot in Auld Reekie again than he is off to a panorama. On the same day, however, he pays one shilling " to the chapel in Edinburgh," and I doubt not that he went there to say a prayer for his sins. Before going home he made some interesting purchases—10 lb. of wax candles from Henderson in South Bridge for twenty-nine shillings; a pair of candlesticks from Ritchie, ironmonger, in the High Street for twenty-nine and twopence; and, one pound for sundries! Oh these slumps in sundry—how they cover, like charity, a multitude of other things! But when he left Simpson's Hotel this time his bill, after four days, is somewhat alarming—" Paid for lodgings, dinner, and three servants, &c., twenty pounds thirteen shillings." The waiter this time got ten shillings, so did the chambermaid, but the boots got half a crown, and the ostler one shilling.

The posting from Edinburgh to Peebles cost him over two pounds; and post-horses from Peebles to his own house at Innerleithen cost nearly another pound. This leads us to conjecture that he posted all the way in his own coach, especially when we remember the pair of large carriage lamps which he provided himself with in London at no little expense. On the other hand, " seven pounds paid for journey

from London to Edinburgh in posting," as he puts
it, would hardly seem to cover the expense of post-
horses for a gentleman's carriage. Robert Scott, the
servant, did not return by road, but by steerage
passage (two pounds twelve and six) on the steam
vessel, which he boarded the very day before his
master set out by road.

But Mary Birch—who was she? Probably the
family governess, who was returning to Tweedside
for the winter, for the laird did not take her with
him in his poste-chaise, but entered into his pass-
book this item—" Paid for an inside place to Peebles
by the coach for Mary Birch."

The very last thing he did in Edinburgh was to
go to Mr Rodger, the hairdresser, and spend five
shillings, which shows us that the laird was dooms
particular about his hair, and must have it dressed
and curled ere he appeared before his women-folks.
When in London he had, like a true Scotsman of
parts, bought three books—a pamphlet on Paul Jones
for sixpence; a copy of La Guia de Torasteros for
1830, for which he paid ten shillings; and the French
spelling-book.

We shall now leave our laird trundling home
alone in his poste-chaise with the high C-springs,
over the October moors by Leadburn, his grey Scots
eyes gleaming with the light of love as he passed
down Eddleston Water by Early Vale and Cringletie,
and in his hand he held the thin, well-thumbed
pamphlet on Paul Jones. When the sun was setting,
he sat looking out of the window of his lumbering
coach to catch the glamour of the after-glow on
Tweed—that storied river of home, which was better

to him than all he had seen at Covent Garden or Vauxhall. For the hardest Scotsman is at heart a sentimentalist.

. . . .

After the above story appeared in *The Scotsman*, I received several letters from Tweedside folk identifying the Border Laird as the last Earl of Traquair, and I was most hospitably entertained at Traquair House. I then found that the only mistake I had made was in supposing that the Earl was a married man with three daughters. The fact was that his sister Lady Louisa Stuart kept house for him, and three nieces lived with them. So, the blue moreen travelling bag and the five guinea shawl were for Lady Louisa, and the three dresses—the print gown at 30s., the buff-coloured gown at 15s., and the pink gown at 13s. were for the three nieces, according to their varying ages.

The Diary came into my possession in a rather strange, round-about way. It was found in the effects of an officer who was killed in the war. His brother, who was related to me by marriage, handed it on to me after the war. On looking into it I realized the interest of it, and wrote " The Diary of a Tweedside Laird a Hundred Years Ago," locating the house to within two miles of Innerleithen. The old Account Book now lies where it ought to be—in the charter chest in Traquair House.

The last Earl died in 1861, and his sister, Lady Louisa Stuart died in 1875. A picture of this quaint old Scots gentlewoman lies before me as I write. Within a very short time of her death, she insisted on posting to Edinburgh to buy a new bonnet. It was her last adventure for she contracted a chill and died immediately after, in her hundredth year.

.   .   .   .

How often have I gazed through the old gates with the Bradwardine Bears on the pillars, as one might look lovingly on some very old man who has outlived his century, with little twinkling eyes in a face that is all lined and wrinkled with the furrows of time. But perhaps the most picturesque view of the old house is got from the water's side where the Quair burn goes " singin' doon to the vale o' Tweed," and falls with a quiet gurgle and a swirl of its tail into the river of romance. The house gleams weird and white through the bare trees even in the morning light; but if you came here in the gloaming it would look even more mysterious and ghostly. Four swans float by the river bank. A cushie is crooning in a high tree. The solitude is secure.

Not long ago, I wandered up the old drove road which leads over Minchmoor, and had my lunch on the top of that haunted wilderness between Tweed and Yarrow. The Cheese Well gleamed like a blue eye in the brown heather—clean, cool, and still, like a good life. On the way up I met an old man near the pine wood, and passed the time of day with him.

On this moor I always think of four Scotsmen— the Great Marquis; Sir Walter Scott, who said good- bye to Mungo Park over yonder on Williamshope Ridge; James Hogg, the Ettrick Shepherd, who laid the scene of " Bonny Kilmany " in Plora Wood,

having lifted a local legend of a child stolen by the
fairies from Satyr Sykes in Traquair; and Dr John
Brown, whose non-such paper on " Minchmoor " first
filled me with a strong desire to cross this drove
road.

As I lay on my back on the heather gazing up into
the blue sky, I heard the " peching " of desperate
men and the jingle of horses' bits as a little company
of troopers cantered on the turf. After the defeat
of Philiphaugh, the first fugitives made their way
over this road. The Earl of Traquair was a follower
of Montrose and a King's man. But he was an
inveterate " trimmer," and was trusted neither by
Cavalier nor by Covenanter. So in 1645 he sent his
son, Lord Linton, with a troop of horse to join
Montrose. But, for some reason or other, the
troop withdrew before the Battle of Philiphaugh.
Treachery was suspected, but it was never proved.

When Montrose was making his way over Minchmoor, he naturally drew rein at the door of Traquair
House. With him were a few trusted friends—the
two Napiers, Lord Erskine, Lord Fleming, Dalziel,
and Douglas. When Montrose knocked at the door
of Traquair the Earl and his son were both within.
But they " denied themselves," as the phrase nicely
puts it, and the Marquis, turning away from the
closed door, made his way up Tweed by Peebles,
Manor, and Stobo to Biggar. When, however, the
victorious Leslie, with Argyle and Lothian, arrived
at Traquair later on in pursuit of Montrose, the
cat-jumping Earl opened the door and welcomed
them.

The only time I put my hand on the door with

its iron studs, ere I passed through it, I thought of Montrose with a twist of pain. For, whatever be our sides in the quarrels of kings or commoners, we can never forgive a betrayal of friendship.

When I came down to the tiny village and was about to walk to Innerleithen, I met the old man to whom I had spoken on the drove road. He was walking slowly towards the bridge over the Quair burn. So I turned and joined him, and we made for the Bradwardine Bears. He was a native of Traquair, and had lived for nearly thirty years in Kent and the New Forest. But, like many another exiled Scot, he had come back to spend his last days in the Tweedside village where he had been born. I asked him if he lived in the house where he was born. "No," he replied, "I was born in the tapmaist hoose, but noo I bide in the laigh-maist."

And his word was a symbol of his long life.

He remembered Lady Louisa. In those days there were many more houses in the parish, with a few weavers, and a tailor who lived at the Gates. Now the gatehouse where the weaver lived is tenantless, and the roof of the other lodge is "sairly seggit." It is said that after the defeat of Prince Charles Edward at Culloden the Stuarts of Traquair vowed that the Gates would never be opened again until another Stuart King was on the throne. But my old friend remembers as a boy seeing the Gates opened by the local smith who had to repair one of them. He pointed out the very bit of wrought iron which had been renewed, and we examined it together.

What a heartsome thing it is to wander along a
road with an old man, holding collogue with him
about bygone days, and the little odd scraps of news
which will never find their way into the history
books!

V

GANGREL'S GLORY

A DAY ON FRUID

WE are often advised to live dangerously. But, if a prophet were to arise to-day, he would probably advise us to make an effort to live peacefully. Our danger is speed, rush, hurry, and that egotistic intensity which scoffs at tranquillity.

I hope I am no coward. But I have come to believe in the necessity of running away occasionally. For the man who cannot stop working is already ill. And he who never gets out of his own ego and has a good laugh at himself has already lost his humour.

One June morning the car dropped me at Tweedsmuir roadend. It is a tiny clachan with a kirk. An Edinburgh bailie probably associates Tweedsmuir with an annual inspection of Talla Waterworks. The ordinary motorist whisks past it with a pitying thought of god-forsakenness. But some of us know better, for to us it is the gateway to many haunts of happiness.

I made my way through the clachan, with a glance over the parapets of Tweed Bridge, and past the three great stones to Menzion—only, we call it Mingan. At the back of the farmhouse a roadman was napping stones—the most moral of all trades,

for a roadman is always mending his own ways and
the ways of other people as well.   From the shoulder
of the hill as you pass into the Fruid Valley you get
a fine view of Upper Tweed.   The hills round about
Fruid are green to the top, making an ideal sheep
walk, with a quiet stream which flows all the more
slowly because the glen is almost level.

I wonder if there is any country in the world
where the men of it grow so fond of the bird music
of the moors!   Larks were soaring up into the blue
as I wandered on, bursting their throats with the
melody they threw down on the earth.   The elusive
notes of that wandering voice, the cuckoo, came
softly from the distant Tweed.   Golden plovers
whistled occasionally on the heather. But the whaup,
king of all moorland birds, held the hills.

All through my life the whaup has been my
favourite bird, the noisy grey curlew, with a six-inch
beak that is curved like a bow.   There is something
uncanny about its constant *cour-lieu, cour-lieu.*   But
there are many notes in whaup music.

There is first of all the low, quiet whistle with a
rising inflection in it, repeated again and again, and
often ending there with no more ado.   Then there
is the full call, beginning with the low, quiet tones,
but gradually bursting into the glamorous gurl which
literally fills the glen and the heart of the moorland
lover with a sense of rapturous joy, which, when it
has spent itself, dies away in sad complaint, like the
sigh of a lost soul coming down the wind in the
gloaming of the summer night.

Add to these the *whittering,* or the *wheeple,* when
alarmed.   For the whaup in nesting time flies about

giving forth an excited nervous note, concerned like all good parents for the safety of its young. The whittering or wheepling whaup is an anxious bird. Last of all, when flying very high the whaup has a strange double call—*whit too, whit too*—the last note with a long rise and fall in it.

The call of the whaup is sometimes painfully human. I have heard a whaup crying quietly at night-fall, like a broken-hearted child. And when it comes to poetry, no one has described this king of moorland birds so poignantly as Robert Wanlock Reid in his poem " The Whaup," which you will find printed on page 118.

These words were written by an exiled Scot, and there are some of his kind in every corner of the earth who would give anything to hear the gurl of a whaup on the hills of home again.

The golden plover is an intriguing bird. Not so accessible as its near relation the green plover, or lapwing—or, as we call it, the peesweep. The golden plover is well called " the whistler," from its repeated liquid call. You find these birds on the upper moors rather than on the lower fields where the lapwings are. The normal call of the golden plover is a clear *tlu*. These birds are inveterate concealers of their nests, and first-rate playactors. How often have I stalked one in early summer, or concealed myself behind a heather knoll with a pair of field glasses to watch a plover keeping sentry over the nest near by, and to whistle an answer to every *tlu* it made! But if you follow it quietly over the moor, the wily bird will not take to the wing, but will run as closely and as swiftly over the heather as a rat, leading you further away from the nest, and only taking flight when you get perilously near to it. The tiny plovers, when hatched, are like little yellow balls of fluff.

The more bird friends you have, and the more knowledge of bird music you gain, the less lonely will you feel on moorland or hill, and the oftener you will wish to be there.

Standing the next day on a hilltop between Tweed and Kingledoors, I got an incomparable view, before a sudden mist came on. Behind me rose Culter Fell. In front was Talla, lying like an oblong silver mirror among the tawny hills. Behind Fruid rose Hart Fell, and as I swept my eye northwards I picked up the masses of Broadlaw, Dollar Law and Scrape.

In some ways the hill climber has the advantages of the airman. He looks down on the map of the world, and picks out details which a walker or motorist cannot possibly see. Yonder, for example, on the further side of Tweed, are the green ramparts of Chester Lees Fort, which I walked over yesterday. Seen from this hilltop, it is as clean a circle as any of the little stells in the hirsels. And yet the downward view of things can be very disappointing. Only once have I been in an aeroplane, and we flew up and down a stretch of Tweed. Alas, this Queen of Rivers appeared to me like a tiny ditch, and all my beloved hills were flattened out so that they had no longer any personality or shape left.

When lunch-time came in Fruid I chose the only spot where a wandering man can be securely hidden —on the river side behind a knoll of spruce and pine trees. For there are certain essentials about the perfect lunching place for a gangrel. The first is that it be strictly private. The second is that it have a trout-pool handy. The third is that there must be plenty of sticks for a pine fire whose smoke cannot be detected by prying eyes. The only open view here was to the hillside opposite. But, then, even herds must feed between twelve and one o'clock.

There is a certain gangrel whose methods I have every reason to remember. Sometimes he takes a long cast of fine gut from his pocket and busks it with one lure. More often he just takes off his jacket and waistcoat. Then he lies down and wriggles to the edge of the green bank until his eyes and nose are just overhanging the water. Then, with the cunning of a criminal, he slips his long bare arms slowly and silently into the water, and the sensitive fingers feel for something very soft under the bank. When he has found it there follows a gentle tickle and rub far more tender than the touch of a skilled masseur, until suddenly the fingers grip, and one great wet arm flings the silvery something backwards on the bank. This process is always easier when a friend sits on your heels while you are exploring that under world that is hidden beneath the bank. There have been times when the lonely gangrel in his eagerness has over-balanced himself and plunged head first into the golden stream. But that is only his way of having a cool dip before food.

To continue my friend's methods. By this time the fire is glowing red. The solitary takes an " apple " from his pocket, or, indeed, anything else that may be cookable, and roasts it. The very fragrance makes him hungry.

The last touch of pure pleasure comes at the end of all things, when the scent of good coffee perfumes the air. Taking up a glowing pine runt, he lights his pipe with he finest match in the world, thus adding a flavour to his smoke which a millionaire could not buy for money. That day I left the pine knoll in Fruid and a little heap of dead ashes with great regret. But I often think of gangrel's glory when I am in very different circumstances.

I followed the bank of the stream down again. There were long, lazy pools that were as calm as a mirror, with nothing to break the thrum of peace but the plop of little trout. The white *canach* or cotton grass grew in the bogs. Lady's mantle trailed green skirts in the water where the plants overhung the stream. The grassy banks were full of purple violets, yellow tormentilla, and blue speedwells. Summer happiness demands flowers as well as birds.

And yet, if you linger long enough in solitary places, you will find the human touch, which is better than all landscape.

The first time I was plugging down the Fruid on a sweltering hot day in June I came upon a stout motherly woman wheeling a bicycle up one of the steep little rises on the road. I offered to wheel the bicycle for her, and we so got on the crack. One thing I shall never forget. She cycled down Fruid for three miles with her little boy to school at Tweedsmuir in the morning; cycled home again; cycled down once more for him in the afternoon, and cycled back with him. Twelve miles daily, except in bad weather, when he did not go! Add to that her ordinary housekeeping, and how many modern mothers would like to change places with her?

On this occasion I saw a man coming up the road, so I left the trout stream and met him as if by chance. He was the kind of man you never see on Princes Street. A little country man, with a happy twinkle in his blue eyes; a very red sunburnt face; old clothes which blended with the landscape; a poke on his back which doubtless contained all his other duds; and a little shepherd's crook in his right hand. I began with the weather, but he replied about trout.

"Have ye been fishin'?"

"How can a man fish without a rod," I replied, "and the water is very low."

"Aye, so I see. Weel, I killed a weasel doon the road."

"A whutterick! Were you not afraid that the brute would turn on you?"

"No me. I never gi'ed it a chance. He was makin' for a wee rabbit that was squealin' wi' fricht."

"And how did you do it?"

"Wi' my stick."

For a rabbit is paralysed with terror on the approach of a weasel, just as a bird is paralysed by a snake.

"I never gi'ed him a chance."

Could anyone better describe the instinctive action of a sportsman?

And I thought of David Harum, and his horse dealer's invariable rule—"Do to the other fellow what he wants to do to you—only—do it first."

We parted, and I found the weasel half a mile down the road. A beautiful specimen, with little or no sign of the sharp tap of the old stick. I took out my steel tape and measured it—seven or eight inches long in all. Its back and tail and top of the head a beautiful brown, and its belly, little legs, and under part of the face pure white, with a firm but wicked little mouth. So small and beautiful, but such a cruel little devil when it comes to a kill.

When I got down to Tweedsmuir on my way to The Crook, I saw six boys working at little specimen beds in the school garden under the tuition of the schoolmaster. Could one of them be the little fellow that used to give his mother a twelve-miles run down Fruid every summer day?

VI

LONELY LOITERING

IN UPPER TWEEDSIDE

EVERY river has its own beauty, and to me the Tweed will always remain like no other river in Scotland. From source to sea it is a haunted stream. Its holms and hills and lonely glens are steeped in the romance of centuries. None knew that better than Andrew Lang and the poets who wrote about Tweed from their innermost hearts.

Those who prefer a dash of dour Lowland prose will find it in one of John Buchan's early books, where he makes Nicol Plenderleith say: —

" I aye turn fair sick for the smell o' moss and heather, and the roarin' and routin' o' the burn, and the air sae clean and snell that it gars yer face prick and yer legs and airms strauchten oot till ye think ye could rin frae here to the Heids o' Ayr. . . . And if I micht choose the place I wad best like to dee in, it wad be at the lee side o' a muckle hill, wi' nae death bed or sic like clavers, but juist to gang straucht to my Makker frae the yirth I aye traivelled on."

In heavenly June weather I took the way up Tweed from Broughton to Tweedsmuir. On the Moffat road there is now a constant stream of cars.

But, while you may *look* at any countryside while travelling in a car, you can never hope to *see* it— and there is all the difference between looking and seeing. To see any place you must know it: to know it you must love it: and to love it is to loiter in it. Main roads are all very well. But it is in the byways and up the lonely little glens that you will come on all that makes a countryside worth while.

The first step aside after leaving Broughton is the old road that leads to Kilbucho. My first visit made me fall in love with Kilbucho Place—a tall, white house with an indescribable Scots dignity about it and great possibilities. Ever since, I have dreamed of it as one might dream of a castle in Spain. It was a still afternoon when I set out to visit Kilbucho Kirk. I sat high up on the old Biggar road and looked down on a clump of trees. Among these trees I knew there stood the ruined kirk, with what was once the manse close by. The kirk is but a rickle of ruined walls now, but the manse is still a private dwelling-house. So, down I went, and there in the gloom of a planting stood the grey ghost of a sanctuary.

There is plenty of history about the place for anyone who likes to dig it up. But it is so easy to drive away the spirit of any place by raking up every bone you can find. Enough for me to remember as I wandered about this sacred grove that as far back as 1233 a pious lady, the daughter of a knight, sold land and bought masses for herself and the souls of the two parsons of Kilbucho who were called Gilbert and Gamelin. There is also a rather comical entry in the Records of 1628 which tells us that John Thriepland muttered and whispered to the congregation during sermon, spoke back to the minister when ordered to be silent, and even followed the minister with weapons and wanted to fight him!

Kilbucho was the *kil* or Church of Begha, the saintly daughter of an Irish prince, who fled for her soul's sake to Scotland and worked with St Hilda under the great Aidan, in the seventh century. Somewhere nearby is a well of St Bee's or St Begha, and you may still walk on the beautiful green banks which the monks threw up at great labour.

A mile or so further up the Moffat road take the first turn to the right and you will find yourself at the entrance of another of the most beautiful little glens in Tweedside—Holms Water. Near the foot of this valley there is a school, a house or two, and the old graveyard of Glenholm Church. It is a beautifully kept Godsacre, with the Holms Water murmuring past it, and ancient trees bielding the sleeping dead. The finely situated house of Quarter looks down on the peaceful scene from a wooded slope on the further side.

Here is the burial-place of the Tweedies of Quarter, adorned by the family arms—a lion rampant holding an anchor of hope, with this truly Scots motto below: *Thole and think on!* What a combine of patience, strength, and good Scots silence, with a rebuke to all wordy complaints!

Another stone bears a remarkable memorial to a well-beloved student: " Erected by subscription to the memory of William Steven, who died at Holms Mill on the tenth of June 1828: —

His was a heart
Devoid of guile;
Tho' Master of Art
They did him style;
You that are bent
To get to heaven
Be innocent
Like Willie Steven.

A homely tribute to a good life; and what a world of affection there is in the " Willie."

This church of Glenholm, like the chapel of Kingledoors further up Tweed, was dedicated to St Cuthbert. But there is only one angle of the wall left, all ivy-covered, with the tombstone of an old minister on the gable end.

The walk up Holms Water takes you right into the heart of a typical glen of Tweed—green sheep holms by the river, fine feeding on the lower slopes, and heather hills hemming you in on every side, with the great mass of Culter Fell guarding the glen-head. I followed the road up to Glencotho Lodge—surely one of the sweetest little lodges on Tweedside, with dazzling white walls and well-kept turf. Here I foregathered with the shepherd, went in, and spent one of those happy hours which can turn strangers into friends and discover intimacies that are sealed by many a surprise of mutual acquaintance. Only those who take some opportunity of leisure can explore such sequestered vales of life, where dwell the sons and daughters of toil who enjoy the harvest of a quiet eye, and serve their generation in abundance of peace.

Striking up the cleuch to the left, I followed the rough path right over the heather-tops into Kingledoors valley. By the still waters and green pastures of Glenholm I had gathered riches that are better than gold.

From the top of the hill, the rounded summits of Culter Fell, Scrape, Dollar Law, and many a lesser height, rolled away from horizon to horizon like a brown-billowed sea. The heat was intense. Down in the valley the white lodge of Kingledoors snuggled among the trees. Thunder muttered away to the south, but the caller north wind kept on blowing as I dropped down the hill and was soon in the cool tunnel of the Kingledoors avenue.

Let no lover of Tweedside neglect Kingledoors. On another day of great heat I climbed over the hills from Tweedsmuir into the upper part of Kingledoors glen, where I wandered happily, and in utter solitude, for most of the day. There is a certain long pool in the river which circles round a bank. The water is of a clear, golden colour, and I found it irresistible. I refer to no nefarious lures. But, sitting on the bank, I remembered that one of our illustrious authorities on Scots place names has derived Kingle-doors from three Gaelic words—*Ceann, gill, dobhair*—meaning the Head of the Clear Water. That settled it. I shed all the conventions of civilisation, and was soon lying with only the head above the clear water, at perfect peace, listening to the music of a wonderful world—whaups gurling in the sky, sheep baaing on the hill, and the sound of the stream running over stones.

There is a notice on the roadside near Logan Burn which must puzzle many motorists and hikers—" Site of Lincumdoddie." Here stood the cottage

referred to by Robert Burns in his song of " Willie
Wastle." Willie was remembered by that most
awful of all memorials—an impossible wife.

> Willie Wastle dwalt on Tweed
>   The spot they ca'd it Lincumdoddie;
> Willie was a wabster guid
>   Could stown a clue wi ony body.
> He had a wife was dour and din,
>   O Tinkler Madgie was her mither.
>
> .   .   .   .   .   .
>
> She has an ee, she has but ane,
>   The cat has twa the very colour;
> Five rusty teeth, forbye a stump,
>   A clapper tongue wad deave a miller;
> A whiskin beard about her mou,
>   Her nose and chin they threaten ither.
> Sic a wife as Willie had,
>   I wad na gie a button for her.

There is more than that in the poem, and worse.
Surely Burns must have suffered badly at the hands
of this eldritch woman, else he would never have
poured such scorn on her.

Then comes Polmood, a house buried in trees
across the Tweed. There is a curiously worded
charter concerning Polmood which I find quoted in
an old book on the district. But it is too good to be
true:

" I, Malcolm Canmore, king, the first of my reign, give
to thee Norman Hunter of Powmood, the Hope up and
down, above the earth to Heaven and below the earth to
Hell, as free to thee and thine as ever God gave it to me
and mine, and that for a Bow and a Broad Arrow when
I come to hunt in Yarrow; and for the mair sooth I bite
the white wax with my tooth, before thir witnesses three,
May, Mauld, and Marjorie."

With that terrific piece of legality mixed with prosy poetry, more false than true on the face of it, I fear, we reach the Crook Inn. Here is the ideal place to stay when exploring this district. Even standing on the doorstep of the Crook Inn, there is something to see. Right opposite, on the other side of the road, lies the garden of the Inn surrounded by trees. Look at the garden wall. It is only a drystane dyke. But it is one of the finest specimens in Scotland of an almost lost art. It is built of flat stones fitted to perfection, without a chink or hole appearing, and it is finished on the top with rougher stones as it should be. I wonder who built it, and when it was built? At least, it is the memorial of a good workman that needeth not to be ashamed.

No one can wander about Tweedsmuir without dreaming of the Covenanters, and wherever you go you will have the stillness of sheep-hills for company and little trout pools for pleasure.

In the middle of June 1682 Claverhouse was nearly trapped by a company of Hillmen at the Bield. They had been holding their quarterly conventicle at Talla Linns, where they had passed a resolution to send Earlston to Holland; disclaiming any connection with James Russell, who urged the non-payment of tolls and customs; and even discussing the reliability of the elusive Peden. To-day at Talla Linns the silence is only broken by the sound of running water. But if you have an ear for the sad music of the Killing Times you will hear the notes of a psalm coming downhill on the breeze.

In Tweedsmuir Churchyard you will find a martyr's stone.

" Here lyes John Hunter, martyr, who was cruely murdered at Corehead by Col. Jas. Douglas and his party for his adherence to the Word of God and Scotland's Covenanted Work of Reformation—1685. Erected in the year 1726."

On the other side of the stone is carved an extract from a contemporary record which tells the story. The lad was visiting a sick friend at Corehead when he was surprised by the dragoons. He fled over the hills, but a dragoon named Scott rounded him up and shot him through the body. He then struck him over the head and threw him down a steep craig.

In this churchyard there is a modern tombstone which should interest every Edinburgh citizen: " To the memory of the men who died during the progress of the Talla Water Works, 1895-1905, of whom over thirty are interred in this churchyard. Erected by their fellow-workmen."

Here, also, is the burial-place of the Kers of Tweedshaws, one of whom, the Rev. Professor John Ker, D.D., Edinburgh, was born at The Bield, the white house over the river yonder on the Moffat road. On the gable end there is a little bronze tablet commemorating this poet, preacher, and professor.

Last of all, when you have explored Menzion Water and Fruid Water, if you would complete the pilgrimage to Upper Tweedside, you must travel to the summit of the road beyond Tweedshaws, where you will find a notice-board directing you to Tweed's Well, the source of the Tweed. In this clear, cold, overflowing well, 1250 feet above the sea and eighty-seven miles from Berwick, the most romantic river in Scotland has its modest beginning. Many a time

I look at Sir George Reid's beautiful drawing of Tweed's Well in the dark winter days, and think of the little Corse Burn; of Tweed's Cross which stood on the ancient road across the watershed at Corse Dod; and of the border raiders galloping over it from Annandale into Tweedside. On the south side of the watershed rises the Annan, which pours its waters into the Solway Firth. Yonder to the north-west is Clyde Law, where the infant Clyde trickles down the hillside and after travelling 106 miles bears on its mighty bosom the argosies of the world. And here is Tweed rising like a miracle out of a mountain spring to be lost at last in the great North Sea.

Let no Scotsman try to describe Tweed's Well so long as he can sit down by its side and mutter the words of Dr John Brown: —

"There it is, ever the same, self-contained, all-sufficient; needing no outward help from stream or shower, but fed from its own unseen unfailing spring. In summer when all things are faint with the fierce heat, you may see it lying in the dim waste, a daylight star, in the blaze of the sun, keeping fresh its circle of young grass and flowers. . . . In winter, of all waters it alone lives; the keen ice that seals up and silences the brooks and shallows has no power here. Still it cherishes the same grass and flowers with its secret heat, keeping them in perpetual beauty with its soft warm breath. . . . Pray that you have a heart like this well, full, deep, clear, unchangeable, with Truth at the bottom. . . . In the time of hot raging passion, a fountain of coolness. In shivering grief and bleak misery, a refuge from the storm, a covert from the tempest. . . . Fearless alike of fire or frost. Cool, not cold. Warm, not hot."

E

VII

THE LAND OF MERLIN

A BEND OF TWEED

How many thousands pass down Tweedside every summer without giving themselves time to drink in the beauty, to wander from pool to pool, or to dig out the ancient tales of love and war!

Every Tweedside lover has his own favourite beat on the river. Mine begins at Tweeds Well and ends at Berwick. For the whole river is one long ballad of romance.

From Broughton to Lyne is but a few miles by road. But, apart from the fact that there is no ruined abbey on the riverside, there is no element of Tweedside glory but you will find it here—purple heather hills, green holms, ancient trees, ruined castles of warring Border families, holy cells of the saints, battlefields, and raiders' roads. But the unutterable beauty of Tweedside has outlived everything else.

I have long since given up dogmatising about the finest view in Scotland. The competition is an impossible one. So with Tweed. Those who love it best love it all. And yet, a Scot who rushes down from Broughton to Lyne by the usual road, and never takes it leisurely over the high road by Dreva, misses one of the most moving views in the whole course of this river of romance.

Let us begin then at Tweed's Ford, where an old road crosses the river a little below Mossfennan, and very soon you will find yourself at the ruined castle of Drumelzier, one of the old homes of the Tweedies. But let no man think that because we take this way we are turning our backs willingly on Broughton. Indeed, if anyone has steeped his soul in the family histories of the district—Tweedies of Wrae, Bertram of Duckpool, Geddes of Rachan, Murray and MacQueen of Broughton—memories will at once be stirred of fell fighters, of a gangrel King, of a Jacobite traitor, of a hanging Judge, and of the bitter little wars of the Tweedside clans. Indeed, if you only travelled a mile a day in this glamorous district you would even then be taigled with history.

There are three places which especially tell the tale of the whole district—Drumelzier, Tinnies, and Dawyck. The records of the parish kirks are vital for the story. And if you add the names of Merlin, Kentigern, and Cuthbert, you will not miss much when all is done.

I found Drumelzier Castle a tall ruin standing in a stackyard above a bend of Tweed. Its crumbling walls, with their old shotholes and eyeless windows, are almost hidden from the traveller by the stacks and the ancient trees. Its little courtyard is given over to nettles and hens, and the castle is now the mere adjunct to a pleasant farmhouse. As I stood within the ruined walls and looked up, I could trace the little rooms on the various floors. Outby, I listened to Tweed murmuring its song of peace as it flowed crystal-clear round a gleaming bank of shingle.

This was once the home of the Tweedies of Drumelzier, a wild family whose bitter feuds are long over. The lands belonged first to the Frasers, who seem to have lost them to the Tweedies in the fourteenth century. The Tweedies were a gey family in the time of the Scots Kings. The first was Finlay de Twedyn in Lanarkshire, who lived there in the time of the War of Independence. His grandson appears in 1331 as William Tweedie, Baron of Drumelzier. Perhaps the reason why this family was so renowned for fierce fighting was that they claimed to be descended from a god. For the legend has it that when one of the first Tweedies was away at the Crusades his young wife was wandering by the riverside, and met the god of the stream, who came out of the water and claimed her for his lover. When Tweedie came home be found that his wife had borne a sturdy boy, who became the ancestor of the wild lairds of Drumelzier.

As I walked past the door of the manse and into the Kirkyard of Drumelzier I looked in at the windows, and saw the rooms deserted, as if they had been suddenly left. And so they had. The minister was dead, and the parish was vacant. There was an eerie sense of ghosts about these silent, furnished rooms. In the godsacre itself there was an old man cutting grass with a scythe. I stood afar off and watched him at work. Here was a perfect poem of Time. The church itself is a plain, seemly, Scots kirk, and one would not suspect that it was a pre-Reformation building were it not for the trefoil-

shaped piscina at the east end. On the south side
of what was once the chancel there is now a burial
vault with the Tweedie arms outside. At one time
this vault was the only manse of the parson of
Drumelzier. What troublers those Tweedies must
have been! They swooped down from their castles
of Dreva and Tinnies, and preyed like eagles on the
homesteads in the valley. They defied the Presbytery and the Church, and appeared before the King
and the Lords of the Secret Council. No one,
however, was exempt in those days from the
discipline of the Kirk, and while the Tweedies might
rob the ministers of Drumelzier, Stobo, and Dawyck
on week-days, they were the most frequent culprits
on the stool of repentance within the kirk on Sundays.

Thinking about all these things I stood once more
among the graves and listened. The only sounds
were the sweesh of the scythe, the murmur of the
Powsail Burn below the trees, and the song of a
robin as it piped its plaintive litany. Surely here
was the very essence of man's mortality, with the
dour comment of the Tweedies up yonder on the
stone panel—" Thole and Think."

So I slipped away and started down the Powsail
Burn to visit Merlin's grave on a green holm of
Tweed. Of course, there is no actual grave. But,
what matters that! There is a sough of tradition
that on this very haugh Merlin, the pagan bard, was
stoned to death and buried.

Merlin is the real genius of Drumelzier. Drumelzier means the Ridge of Meldred, a pagan prince
of the district. And it was Meldred's shepherds that
slew Merlin the bard. The heathen bard was present

at the battle of Arthuret in the year 573, when the Christian army gained a victory over the Heathen Host. Merlin fled to the forest of Caledon at Drumelzier, and there ever after the old Druid spent his life among the wild hills with a repute for insanity. This poet priest was doubtless heart-broken at the defeat of has pagan friends. The old order was changing. But the Christian king had brought his friend, St Kentigern or Mungo, to preach the Gospel in upper Tweedside at Stobo. One day Kentigern met a weird-looking man and demanded who he was. " Once I was the prophet of Vortigern (Gwendollen). My name is Merlin. Now I am in these solitudes enduring many privations."

So Kentigern preached the Gospel to the old nature worshipper, and won him to Christ. Up yonder, at the east end of the Dreva road, you will find the rude Altar Stone, where, it is said, Kentigern received the Druid into the Christian Church and dispensed the Sacrament. But, in those dark days of the Faith, the Druids and their Pagan adherents fought hard against the new religion. So, immediately after the admission of Merlin to the Church, the shepherds of Meldred sought him out, stoned him to death on the haughs of Drumelzier, and there, where the Powsail Burn falls quietly into Tweed, Merlin the Martyr was buried. For long his grave was marked by a hawthorn tree.

I sat down in the sunshine by the Powsail Burn to eat my bread and cheese and watch the little trout making eternal circles in the calm water. As I looked across to the Altar Stone on Dreva, I remembered a famous phrase of St Columba which showed how

wisely these early saints in Scotland grafted the New
Faith on to the old nature worship of the Druids—
" My Druid is Christ the Son of God."

There was a curious old prophecy about Merlin's
grave and the Powsail Burn:

When Tweed and Powsail meet at Merlin's Grave,
England and Scotland shall one monarch have.

Strange to say, on the very day that James VI. of
Scotland became James I. of England there was a
terrific flood. Tweed and Powsail overflowed their
banks, and made a new junction at Merlin's grave.

The next objective for a wanderer with a
historical curiosity is Tinnes Castle. The ruins of
this stronghold stand on the summit of a very steep,
detached green hill on the south bank of Tweed
overlooking Drumelzier Haugh. You pech up a
steep path which winds round the hill to the north-
west corner, but before you reach the top you will
realise what an important castle this eyrie of the
Tweedies must have been. None could approach
Tinnes without the risk of getting an arrow through
the heart, for it is defended on three sides by the
extreme steepness of the hill, and on the fourth side
there is a deep gully between the site and the open
heather hills.

Little remains of the castle to-day, for William
Stuart of Traquair destroyed it in the year 1592, by
order of the King. But you can still trace the walls
of the 60-feet square courtyard, and the round
towers which were built at each angle, one of which
still remains in parts. What a magnificent rickle of
old stones Tinnes is to-day! Needless to say, the

view up and down Tweed and across to Dreva is uninterrupted.

Everyone who passed Tinnes, or the Thane's Castle, had to salute and pay homage to the haughty Tweedie. One day James V. passed the castle while on a hunting expedition. Needless to say, he took no notice of the Tweedie. Immediately he was pursued, and taken at Glenwhappen, where the angry thane demanded satisfaction. The King simply blew his hunting horn, and soon the royal retinue surrounded Tweedie and his men. The thane was glad to escape with his life.

If Tweedside is somewhat bare at Drumelzier Haugh, you enter a demesne of sylvan wonders as you step down the road to Dawyck. The first time I plunged through Dawyck woods I came down from the top of Scrape after a long day in Manor. But, in the glorious September weather of this year I not only wandered down the riverside from Tinnes to Dawyck, but came over from Manor by way of the Deid Wife's Grave.

Dawyck doubtless was a bare, bald place when the first member of the Norman French family of Veitch arrived. In 1214 there were present at the adjustment of the marches on Tweedside " Gylmor, the hind of Dauwic," and " Mihhyn, the seneschal of Dauwic." In 1296 William le Vache, of the county of Peebles, swore fealty to Edward I. of England. This man with the French name which means " cow " was succeeded by Barnaba Vache of Dawyck. In 1474 appears William the Vache of Dawic, from whom the family descends without a break. Like the Tweedies, their neighbours and enemies, the

Veitches seem to have been wild and efficient cattle-lifters. One of them was called the " Deil o' Dawyck," a man of mighty strength, from whose sword stroke none ever rose up again.

There is a curious little puzzle in place-names about the Veitches. The name Vache in French means cow. But the name Dawyck in old Celtic means a *Davoch* or *Dawach*, which is a Scots land measure meaning a small district consisting of several ox-gangs. So these old Veitches were really *Cowmen*, and their lands were made up of so many ox-gangs. After that, it is not surprising to find that on their family arms to this day they carry three cows' heads.

In the year 1497 there are two entries in the accounts of the Lord High Treasurer, each for 18s. paid to " ane man of the laird of Dawikkis that brocht quick herounis to the king." The king was James IV., and the herons of Dawyck are still there. I have seldom seen so many herons as I did this summer on Tweedside about Dawyck.

To-day, Dawyck is famous for its magnificent forest trees. The Veitches sold Dawyck to the Naesmyths in 1691. They in turn held the lands till 1897, when they passed to the Balfours. In the time of the Naesmyths many trees were planted. Indeed, the lairds of Dawyck seem to have handed down this love of tree planting, for the present proprietor is an expert botanist, and his collection of trees and shrubs is one of the finest in Scotland.

As you come over the old heather-grown right-of-way from Posso, in Manor, you can almost hear the lowing of cattle beasts and the jingle of horses' bridles. For this is part of the famous old reivers' way, which was called Thieves' Road. On the summit of the hill you pass the Deid Wife's Grave. The story goes that after the defeat of the Great Montrose at Philiphaugh, an Irish soldier and his wife were fleeing westward across the hills, but were overtaken by Leslie's troopers and killed somewhere near this spot, where there is an opening in the boundary dyke. What a view bursts on you as you stand on the summit and gaze! It was evening when I came over, and the whole valley of the Tweed from Broughton Heights and far Tinto lay before me in the golden light. The river glittered between the woods of Dawyck and Stobo, and the peace of heaven seemed to lie over the whole land.

It was a September morning when I said good-bye to Tweedside. We made our way up the Dreva road to the Altar Stone for the last time. There is an old grassy road just below the farm house. A few yards down this road you will find solitude and a wonderful view. Tweed murmured in the silence far beneath us. The mists of morning had already been drunk up by the sun. The wooded slopes of Dawyck were steeped in light, and a column of smoke rose from the half-hidden chimneys of the House of Dawyck. The purple moors swept up to the skyline where the drove road drops over to Manor. Westward up Tweed the blue hills rose against a cloudless sky. The bracken was turning to gold, and here and there the trees were red with the first fires of autumn. The beauty of the world was almost too much at that moment. So we returned to the Altar Stone.

It is a great square boulder with a perfectly flat

top, almost hidden by the greenery of the roadside. You have only to place your hand on the top of this rude altar, shut your eyes, and if you have the gift you will see visions. A weird Druid standing beside a Christian Gospeller—old Merlin, the pagan bard, humbly accepting the Holy Sacrament from the hands of Mungo, the loveable man of Christ. So this shrine of heathen worship became the Altar Stone of the New Faith which was to save mankind. A fair and sacred morning it must have been to Merlin in his old age. But ere night fell on Tweed he was lying on a green haugh across the water, a martyr of Christ, stoned to death.

VIII

THE HOUSE OF QUIET

A TWEEDSIDE RETREAT

It stands high above the river, and well off the main road. Great trees bield it east and west; the sloping lawn in front runs down between them to a little wall that raises it above the green fields; and there is an open view southwards across the Tweed valley to the Manor hills, so that the front of the house basks in the sun. To the west of the house there is a garden enclosed, with grass walks, plums ripening in the sun, roses and flowers making a brave show, and a rustic seat where you can sit and dream, as you listen to the wind in the tree tops and enjoy the lown of a sunny tranquillity.

Behind stands the house of a remoter century with its typical courtyard of outer buildings; and behind that again, the green sheep-walk runs up beyond the pond to the heather hills of Tweed.

The first night I slept in the House of Quiet, a September frost had come. The stars glittered above the hills, and the open windows of the room let in the sweet scents of a world that held in it nothing but God's fragrances. No living creature seemed to be awake, and I murmured to myself ere I fell asleep: —" Did ever anyone hear such silence! "

Even the morning sounds that wake you are full of restfulness—the *chirrup* of partridges in the field; the hollow *kuk-kuk* of a cock pheasant in the trees; the crooning of cushies as they preen themselves in the early morning sun.

Here surely is a blessed retreat from the racket of the city which is only twenty-three miles off.

The House of Quiet stands in the very centre of a multitude of ancient things which take you back to the beginnings of history and long before that.

Down yonder, on the green plateau of Sheriffmuir there stand two great stones, hoary reminders of those Druid magicians who built their stone circles for sun worship and the bloody sacrifice. Across the road in a wood there is a circular hollow locally known as *The Pinkie*, where tradition tells us, the sacrificial procession was formed. Certainly the gloomy hollow is exactly aligned with the two stones. But, no man can now say with certainty what took place in the great stone temples like Stonehenge, Callernish and Stennis; what exactly was the pagan ritual; or what strange use the cup-marked stones were put to. Over yonder at Bellanrig you will find one of these on the roadside, and across the Tweed valley on the heather slopes above Easter Dawyck you will find another. These cup-markings make another insoluble riddle—some explaining the cups by sacrificial ritual, some by sun worship, and others by an ancient astronomical system of star maps.

Thousands of people motor along the road between the Pinkie Hollow and the standing stones on Sheriffmuir and never realize the ghostly significance of the place. On this same Sheriffmuir Edward I.

defeated the Scots, one of whose captains was William
Wallace.

Indeed, you can scarcely take a step from the
House of Quiet without coming on some historic site.
On the right hand side of the road which leads up
to it, there is a large circle of trees with an open
space in the middle. Here stood the ancient tower
of the Frasers of Oliver and Neidpath. It is still
called the Castle Knowe.

I can sit at the door in the sun and count a number
of sites of British Forts on the neighbouring hills.

On this very land there was one on the Hogshill,
two on Cademuir, other two between Manor and
Dawyck, one at Caersknowe in Stobo, still another up
Lyne Water at Hamildean, and if you continue going
up that stream you will find others at Torbank, at
Wester Happrew, and at Ladyurd. Those primitive
Border fortresses were always round or oval in
shape, nearly always built on the top of hills, but
occasionally on the slope of the hill with their
defensive works thrown up towards the south, the
region from which the conquering legions always
came. They were mere refuges for the people and
their cattle, built high enough above river or
marsh to save the inhabitants from flood or pillage.
Strange to say, no trace of an enclosed water supply
is ever found.

There is a delightful old grass-grown road which
leads from the House of Quiet down to the Lyne
Water. If you follow this road and cross the foot-
bridge you will come to one of the finest examples
of a Roman Camp in Scotland. The *castellum* stands
on a flat plateau or moraine not far from Lyne

Church, and about a hundred feet above the river. This is not the place for a detailed description of the Roman Camp. Sufficient to point out that the north and east sides of the Camp were protected by a morass, and the west and south by the very steep slopes which fall away to the river Lyne. Roman Camps, unlike British Forts, were always square or rectangular in shape, with rounded corners. The variation in the width of the fortifications here was of course determined by the steepness of the slope on the one hand and the marsh on the other.

Wander over this green camp to-day among the nibbling sheep and you will realize that the old motto—" Dwell as if about to depart "—had no meaning for the Romans. They came, they saw, they conquered, and they settled down in Britain for the best part of four hundred years. So this camp at Lyne, when explored in 1901, revealed the remains of streets, walls with buttresses, water cisterns, flues for heating, stone buildings, officers' quarters, gateways, a pit lined with red stone masonry, and all the essentials of a comfortable barracks. Yet, even the Romans had to strike camp sometime before the break up of the Roman Empire in 410 A.D., and to-day, both forts and camps are an ancient dream.

But, the finest testimony in stone which is left in the whole district is the ancient Parish Kirk of Stobo. The Romans came and the Romans departed, but Kentigern or Mungo from the Molindinar Burn at Glasgow followed on their heels in the sixth century, and to this very day St Mungo's name is rooted in the traditions of the district. His church is still the centre of the religious life of the parish. Did he not receive into the Christian Church at Altarstone, a few miles further up Tweed, the pagan bard Merlin? In a field almost adjoining the House of Quiet there was a St Mungo's Well, now, alas, drained away. The little Celtic Cell of St Mungo has been restored and is incorporated for worship within the Kirk of Stobo. For, according to the *Registrum Episcopatus Glasguensis,* Stobo became the property of the Diocese of Glasgow some time after St Mungo's death. The rector of Stobo had a " manse " in the Drygate of Glasgow, and the Bishop had a " palace " on the Stobo burn. Indeed, the land in Stobo was said to belong to " God, St Kentigern and the Bishop of Glasgow."

In the restored Cell a pagan monolith eight feet high, with curious markings on it, is now built into the east wall. For those early missionary monks of Christ often erected their first Churches on the sites of the former pagan places of sacrifice. We know that Pope Gregory instructed the great Augustine on his arrival in England, through a letter sent to Bishop Mellitus, that " *the temples of the idols in that nation ought not to be destroyed . . . for, if those temples are well built, it is requisite that they be converted from the worship of devils to the service of the true God; that the nations, seeing that their temples are not destroyed, may remove error from their hearts, and knowing and adoring the true God may the more freely resort to the places to which they have been accustomed. . . . For, there is no doubt that it is impossible to cut off everything at once from their rude natures; because, he who endeavours to ascend to the highest place rises by degrees or steps, and not by leaps."*

Sitting at worship in Stobo Kirk to-day, I remember that remarkable letter. For the pagan stone is still in the wall as a sign of the carry-over from paganism to Christ. Indeed, for over thirteen hundred years this church has passed through all the stages of Scots religion, from the earliest superstition to the present day simplicities of Presbyterian worship—from paganism to Christianity, from the Celtic to the Roman usage, from Episcopal forms to Presbyterian forms, without any cessation in the religious sacrifice.

There are faint markings on the stones of the west wall of the Cell which indicate, almost certainly, a monk's calendar or almanac of days, one stone having a record of a week's observances and another a month's. In the east wall there is a primitive piscina. Outside in the lower stratum of original stone work, you will find what must have been the primitive door step, worn hollow with the feet of many monks. Passing inside again, you will find two upright memorial slabs built in to the north wall; the one to Magister Robertus Vetch (1473); the other to a nameless knight whose two handed sword may have been used at Bannockburn, while his spirit is seen escaping in the form of a dove which flies up to a heavenly cloud. Between these two slabs there has been preserved what looks like a pagan Altar Stone. The Norman-built chancel and nave have evidently been oriented to suit the previously existing cell.

The medieval tower was added to provide a

F

priest's dwelling in the upper storey, and a refuge
for the people in the lower storey in the event of
a raid. The tower thus served as a border keep, and
when it was built it had no entrance to the sanctuary.

There is a little Leper's Squint at the south-east
corner of the church. You might mistake it for a
piscina if it were not that there is no sign of a basin
with an outlet. But, if you feel the lower side of
the lintel with your fingers, you will find two holes
in it, which will prove that there were once two
upright iron staunchions fixed in the stone work to
guard against any entrance by this pathetic little
window so near the altar. The " squint " being at
such a low level, you can imagine the poor outcast
of a leper kneeling outside the wall of the church to
look through at the priest when he was elevating the
Host.

The two tiny Norman windows on the north side
of the chancel; the canopied recess of the Bishop's
tomb from which the effigy was torn at the Reformation; the defaced arms of Glasgow which are still
traceable above; the primitive Norman arch through
which you pass on entering the church—all
these ancient things are doubly dear to a reverent
worshipper.

On the jamb of the old Flodden Porch you can
see the marks made by the local bowmen when
sharpening their arrow points, reminding us of the
days after Flodden when it was ordained by law that
the parishioners were to practise archery in every
churchyard after service. The iron jougs, too, which
were once used to quell the rage of scolding wives,
are still hanging on the left hand side of the porch.

So complete an epitome of the history of the Church in Scotland is Stobo Kirk to-day.

Even the House of Quiet has played some part in the ecclesiastical history of Stobo; for in the old farm house, which still exists as a dwelling place, the Presbyteries of Biggar and Peebles used to meet. Indeed, in 1688 the ministers constituted themselves into the first Presbytery under the Revolution Settlement, and the Rev. William Russell (1689-1699) was ordained in the old farm house of Easter Happrew, not in the Church of Stobo, possibly because the church was still held by the Episcopal incumbent.

One last link with the past.

The Black Dwarf, David Ritchie, was born in a cottage at the House of Quiet about 1740. His father was a quarry labourer, and his mother, Annaple Niven, was an overworked and delicate woman. The Dwarf lived most of his life in Manor and was known as " Bowed Davie of the Wuddus," for the Black Dwarf's cottage still stands at Woodhouse. His legs were like cork-screws, but the rest of his body was quite normal, except that he had long and powerful arms and a very thick skull. One wonders what an Orthopædic Surgeon would have made of the Black Dwarf to-day if he had operated on such a child soon after birth. But, that question could only be answered by an examination of the leg bones of David Ritchie which are now deposited in the Royal College of Surgeons, Edinburgh.

The Black Dwarf was often morose, ill-tempered, and sometimes even violent. He had a certain amount of education and read old books of mythology, some of Shenstone's *Pastorals*, and Milton's *Paradise Lost*. He loved flowers, and his little garden was his delight. He even cultivated the fair sex, and on one occasion went up to the manse to be married. The minister, however, refused to perform the ceremony, and the Dwarf never forgave him. He never wore shoes of any kind, for his feet were so mis-shapen that his stumps were always wrapped in old clouts.

On one occasion Adam Ferguson of Hallyards took Sir Walter Scott to see him. The Black Dwarf grinned evilly at Scott, locked the door, and noticing that the Sheriff was lame put his heavy hand on him and said:

" Hae ye ony poo'er? "

Scott denied the charge.

The Dwarf then signalled to his black cat, and immediately that weird creature jumped up on a shelf and glared at the visitors like an evil spirit.

" Ah," said the Dwarf, pointing at the cat, " he has poo'er!"

The interview being over, Dr Ferguson made Davie unlock the door, and the two friends passed out. But, Ferguson noticed that Scott was as pale as ashes, and was trembling in every limb.

David Ritchie died in Manor in 1811, and was buried in the churchyard, where you will find a stone erected to his memory by William and Robert Chambers. In deference to the Black Dwarf's oft repeated desire, a rowan tree was planted over his grave to keep off the warlocks and the witches.

MELROSE, CLOISTER DOORWAY

IX

FOUR ABBEYS OF THE SAIR SANCT

MELROSE, DRYBURGH, JEDBURGH, KELSO

THE way that leads to the Four Abbeys is indeed a glamorous road. To an Edinburgh man, Eddleston Water is the historic outgait to the Borders and the true pilgrim's path to Scotland's rivers of romance. From Peebles to Abbotsford is twenty miles of the best that Tweed can offer. But as a lover always finds it hard to keep from dwelling on the beauties of his sweetheart's face, so, to a worshipper of Tweed's storied vale, it is hard to refrain from telling those tales of old romance which cling to every castle and cothouse. Traquair, Elibank, Ashiestiel, Fairnilee, Yair, Abbotsford—what tales of the Jacobites, Muckle-mouthed Meg, Alison Rutherford, proud Pringles and the Great Romancer these old houses could tell if only stones could speak! Over the doorway of every one might be written—

The glory dies not, and the grief is past.

In the very heart of this pleasant Border land stands Melrose, and in the very heart of Melrose stands the ruined Abbey—the first of those four which David I. saw rising from the river sides of the Border in his day and generation.

David was the third son of saintly Queen Margaret, that beauty-loving mother, who gave her Royal boys a bias for religion. He was the greatest patron of Cathedral builders that ever reigned in Scotland. To-day, after nearly seven hundred years, we can still see the splendid ruins of no fewer than nine abbeys which were built during his reign as homes for the monks—Kelso, Dryburgh, Melrose, Newbattle, Dundrennan, Kynloss, Cambuskenneth, Holyrood, and Jedburgh. A kind friend to Holy Church was David I. Indeed, so much money did he lavish on these abbeys that for many a year the Kings of Scotland were impoverished. Even three hundred years after the death of the Cathedral builder, James I. shook his head as he stood before his pious predecessor's tomb in Dunfermline and called him " a sair sanct for the croon."

No wise man would try to describe a Cathedral in a paragraph. But surely Melrose Abbey is the finest ruin of David's magnificent unthrift! Standing in rather unromantic surroundings, with the houses of the modern town huddled about it, and almost smothering its beauties, Melrose is a perfect dream in stone. But it was not on this site that the first church stood. Long before David's time, when St Aidan came from Iona in the middle of the seventh century, and set up a Columban community on the Northumbrian Isle of Lindesfarne, he chose twelve Saxon youths and sent them out to preach to the people of these north lands. One of them was Eata, and he was chosen to be the first abbot of the little chapel which was built at Old Melrose on that beautiful green promontory round which Tweed flows so peacefully, far below the incomparable viewpoint of Bemersyde Hill.

But Kenneth the King of Scots burned the little monastery in 839, and, although it was rebuilt, it gradually declined with the fading glories of Iona, until in the eleventh century it was a deserted ruin. Then came David in 1136, and restored the glory of Old Melrose by building a Cistercian Abbey two miles further up Tweed on the present site. Melrose Abbey, in its ancient splendours, must have been a place of ample solitudes. But to-day the town treads on the skirts of its beauty, and laughing tourists look down on its God's Acre from the windows of a neighbouring hotel. Here one seeks in vain for cloistered peace, although it is pleasant to tread the old paths which the restorers have laid bare, with the monks' fountain outlined on its original founds. Despite its modern surroundings, Melrose is the peerless ruin in the Borders. Gazing up at its wonderful traceries, its graceful shafts and its weathered walls, which are all mellowed into a harmony of the softest pinks and greys, yellows and greens, we wonder what purgatory awaits those English invaders—Hertford, Eure, and Layton— who laid waste this beautiful abbey, which looks, even in its ruins, as if it had been wrought by some fairy's hand.

But there is more to come. So we take the road through Newstead to Leaderfoot Bridge, and climb the steep hill, that brings us to the most moving view of Tweed from Bemersyde—the tranquil loop of the river round Old Melrose below us, Gladsmuir on the right, Ravenswood in the middle distance, and

Melrose, with the Eildon Hills beyond, all glittering
blue and wonderful, as if the Creator's hand had
composed a landscape to surpass all else in the
Borderland.

> Twilight, and Tweed, and Eildon Hill,
>   Fair and thrice fair you be;
> You tell me that the voice is still
>   That should have welcomed me.

There speaks one to whom the remembered beauties
of Tweed made a hurt of love in the heart.

Sweeping down the hill past Bemersyde, we turn
suddenly down to the right, and soon are walking
down the narrow path beneath the trees to Dryburgh.

Dryburgh has not the wonders of Melrose to offer
us, but of all the unspoiled sites of the ancient
Abbeys of the Sair Sanct, here is the most perfect.
A Philistine once said to me in Dryburgh, " It is
very dilapidated!" Doubtless. But even the Venus
of Milo lacks her arms.

Here, indeed, is a place to dream of holy friars
and of the monastic ideal. Tweed whispering beyond
the monks' meadows, ancient trees above, the close-
cropped turf of nave and cloister laid in a mosaic
of summer shadows, the yew trees and cedars bearing
mute testimony to monkish hands that planted them
seven hundred years ago. Surely Hugh de Morville,
who founded this Abbey of St Mary about 1150, and
his wife, Beatrix de Beauchamp, who obtained a
charter of confirmation from David I., had souls for
the beautiful things of peace when they chose
Dryburgh. Then came the monks or Canons regular
from Alnwick, with their coarse black cassocks and

JEDBURGH ABBEY

their woollen capes of white, which gave to them the name of White Friars. We can almost see their white shoulders gleam beneath the trees. Yonder, over the meadows, stood the ancient village near the dovecot. Here were the fish ponds. There are the cellars and kitchens. Down in the dim chapter house is still preserved a holy carving of the *Agnus Dei*. At the cloister doorway is an ancient recess for book-shelves. In the only aisle remaining, sleeps Sir Walter Scott, and close by him, Earl Haig. But it is time to go again, so, reluctant but full of Dryburgh peace, we leave the wizard's tomb.

It is a long straight road from St Boswells Green across Ancrum Moor by Lilliard's Edge to Jedburgh, with Peniel Heugh on the left, dark Ruberslaw on the right, and the far Cheviots lying clear and blue from end to end. Ancrum Moor, with its Roman road, is historic ground. Here the English, on returning from the burning of Melrose in 1545, received a severe check from the Scots, who defeated them with great slaughter. Lilliard, a maid of Teviotdale, maddened by the loss of her lover, entered the battle, and fought until, covered with wounds, she fell. Hence the name of Lilliard's Edge to-day. As we cross the Teviot and run up Jedwater towards the town it is difficult for one who knows the history of this fair-situate burgh to keep from shouting the old war-cry of " Jeddart's here!"

No town in the Borders has been so often " dang doon " by the English and " biggit up " again by the Scots as Jedburgh. As early as the year 950 there was a stronghold here called Judanbyrig. Later on a great castle, with six watch-towers to keep the town, stood on the height where the present prison now stands. Here Kings were born, were married, held Court, and died. In 1118 David founded a priory, which was soon replaced by the glorious pile of an abbey church, dedicated to the Virgin, and placed under Canons regular from the Abbey of St Quentin at Beauvais.

If you view Jedburgh in springtime it is like a green jewel set in a riot of blossoming orchards. If you come again in the autumn the whole valley is dressed in the russet and gold of the dying year. Lying in a sequestered vale within ten miles of the old battle border, this dour burgh town was a constant target for the English arrows and guns. Again and again the place was burned, sacked, battered to the ground. As often as its streets and towers, its Castle and its Abbey were burned, the unconquerable men of Jeddart built them up again. Like wasps in a bike, nothing but fire ever turned them out, but they always came back again to sting and retaliate, to fight and harass their auld enemy the English.

Surrey's savageries in 1523 were superb. Yet with only one man to stand up against every four Englishmen, Jeddart defied him until fire swept the Border breed from the town to the towers, where they continued to fight like fiends. No wonder Surrey wrote to his King: " I fownd the Scottis at this tyme the boldest men and the hottest that ever I sawe. . . . Could 40,000 such men be assembled it would be a dreadful enterprise to withstand them . . . the devyl was that nyght among theym six tymes." But the devil has many shapes in Scotland. For on that same fatal night of 23rd September Surrey lost 800 horses in a mad midnight's stampede. Was it some Jeddart horse-couper that played the devil with the beasts? Two hundred were caught rampaging amid the burning ruins by the women of Jedworth; and the terrified English soldiers, thinking that their own wild horses were the Scots come back to raid their camp in the dark, let loose flights of arrows, and fired off their muskets at the maddened animals. Many of them, frantic with fright and stung with many arrows, dashed over the Scaurs near the town, and were killed.

Even Hertford when he came could not utterly destroy the Abbey. But he burned and wrecked it, and scattered the Brethren, who never again returned to the stately pile, where for four hundred years they had made Jedworth a garden of the Lord, and lived amid orchardlands and gardens despite the constant fear of war's alarms.

The Abbey stands to-day in a splendid position above the Jed, a combination of early Norman, transition Norman, and early Gothic beauties. The choir is the oldest part. Pleasant gardens lie between the Abbey and the river. You may pass into the cloister garth by the old Norman door or by the restored Norman door—the one a dream of crumbling loveliness, the other a clean-cut example of modern work. In a vault which lay outside the church proper, was the old Latin School, kept in later years by a parish dominie, where James Thomson, the poet, and Samuel Rutherford, the reformer, learned their letters.

But whether you view the town and valley from

the top of the Abbey tower, or walk the sunny paths of the cloister garden, or saunter up the splendid nave, there keeps ringing in your ears the old cry of " Jeddart's here! " For, despite the drowsy sleep of Jedworth town to-day, here is a burgh of Border men who have not yet grown soft amid their own fruit trees and gardens.

Jeddart Justice meets you face-to-face in the old Town House. The romance of Queen Mary still clings to the little Scots mansion where she lay at death's door of a raging fever, after her mad, fifty-mile ride to Hermitage to see Bothwell. But Jedburgh is a place of moving memories, even if you never get as far as the old Capon Tree, Fernihirst Castle, high-hung Lintalee, or Ringan Oliver's house at Snailcleuchfoot, up the winding valley of the Jed.

But the road calls again, and now we pass through Crailing and Heiton, on our way to Kelso. There is no more impressive view of any Border town than that which bursts on a traveller as he comes down the hill from Maxwellheugh. In the early months of the year the woods of Springwood Park are white with snowdrops. But in summer the Tweed surely looks more queenly from Kelso Bridge than from any town bridge that spans its hundred and three miles from Tweedswell to Berwick. Up stream you look to lordly Floors Castle, past the meeting of the waters, where Teviot falls into Tweed, a wide and wonderful river scene. Across the bridge stands Kelso town, guarded by the square bluff mass of the Abbey ruins.

A bein, clean place in Kelso, with a dignity all its own. Sleepy if you will, but beautiful for situation,

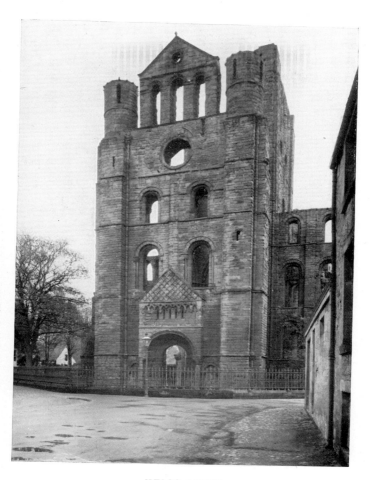

KELSO ABBEY

with spacious river views from the terrace, pleasant gardens, old gentry houses that have well-mannered exteriors, and a market square without an equal in the land. On one side of it a quaint Town House with a pediment and Ionic columns rising out of a graceful balustrade, a cupola with a clock in it to crown the whole, and sweet, lazy chimes to tell the hours without obtruding the flight of time overmuch on the leisurely passers-by. On the other side of the square is an old-world hostelry, where on a market day you will find seated round the sumptuous board lairds and farmers, whose talk is all of horses and hounds, sheep and oats, and other commonalities of a good clean country life. Here might a busy man live his life with some approach to dignity, and enjoy the amenities of a well-earned retiral.

Yet Kelso, too, has known the clash and clang of history. For David placed in this Abbey of the Virgin and St John a Society of Tiron Monks from Picardy about the year 1128, and the Norman tower was constantly used as a defensive keep during the ugly wars of Henry VIII. So it was the old story of hammer and tongs. Dacre gutted the Abbey and burned the town in 1523. Norfolk did the same again in 1542. Hertford completed the ruin two years afterwards.

The Kelso monks, however, were manly fighters. For in that last terrible tulzie with the ruthless Hertford twelve monks and ninety laymen held the Abbey against the English, and when the guns battered down the splendid walls the gallant soldier-monks retreated to the tower, where they held out all night. A dozen Scots escaped by ropes in the darkness, but at dawn the steeple was won, and the last Scot in it died fighting. That was the end.

To-day the only portions remaining are the walls of the north and south-west transepts, part of the western tower, the Galilee porch and one or two pillars. Exiles from Kelso returning home will find the adjoining Abbey house demolished, and a handsome war memorial erected in its place. Is it by chance that in Jedburgh and Kelso the memorials of the Great War are standing alongside of the Abbey ruins? For still these massive towers remain a mute witness to the sad old days of battle, and a lasting reminder that war means death to men and ruin to beauty.

The sun is already casting long shadows, so we turn our faces north again by that high and farhorizoned road which leads us right across the heights by Smailholm village, a sweet, sequestered hamlet on a hill. From Earlston up Leader Vale to Lauder, then over Soutra Hill as the sun begins to set, and back to Edinburgh, with King David's grey citadel on the Rock, and his penitential Abbey of the Holy Rood at the foot of the Royal Mile.

X

WINTER BEAUTY

It is much easier to record facts than to express in writing one flash of beauty. Yet, beauty is one of the supreme facts of life.

"To see, to touch, by ordinary laws is to retain but a point at a time—just the point where you glanced or where your finger fell; weeks of toil it might easily take to acquire and assimilate a scene in that manner. But the imagination, unaccountably stirred, sweeps forward with a sudden billowy swing, gathers an armful in the tick of a moment—and there, before you can wink an eye, is your small laborious treasure increased a hundred fold. . . . When we have learned to create pictures of music, symphonies of fragrance, honey draughts of colour and form, and all in a single achievement of art, then we may hope for an artist with the genius of memory—not till then."

These words from " Earlham " state exactly the despair of every artist in words, colour, or music— this flash of imagination which makes ordinary wayfarers look upon this world and see that wonder in it which is a gift of God to all.

So at least I told myself one February morning when I set out for Tweedside. In this winter of extraordinary mildness, when the sunny north has been able to smile at the fog-bound south, there were days when summer seemed to have wandered by mistake into the midst of winter. The air was still, the skies were blue, the birds had already got over the roughness of their 'prentice notes, and the sun blazed down on the good earth with so much heat in it that it was impossible to wear any kind of overcoat with comfort. The Moorfoots and the Tweedside hills made horizons of the palest amethyst, which met the morning skies in a line so delicate that no artist has ever been able to paint this kiss of colour where earth meets heaven.

The true lover of the country has always known that there are winter beauties which far outshine the more garish beauties of summer. Nor have you to go far to find them.

The ploughed field, for example. You have only to give a sidelong glance over the brown earth, and where there is a hollow in the field you will see the most delicate blues and purples, in the transparent mist which has not yet been drunk up by the heat of the laggard sun. Or look at that long line of unpruned hawthorn hedges. You have only to stand close up to one of them, look along it, and the millions of individual twigs will be blended into a blue mist that is shot through with purples. These blues and purples will never be seen in that field when it is brairded with green, or in that hedgerow when it is in full leafage. And in the lown December days, when the sun shines on the turnip fields, what verdure of summer can compare to the blue-green of the swedes or the livid green of the whites which frame the field in dazzling emerald?

I always associate fairies with a birch wood. There is a little birchen coppice on a bit of swampy ground by the side of the Haystoun avenue. In the distance it looked like another cloud of blue mist. But as I drew near there was a gleam of silver barks, and the little white trunks receded further and further into the blue mist, like an army of tiny elves standing quite still to watch the intruder who had disturbed them at their winter games.

Across the Tweed, the larch woods were sleeping in the sunshine on the rounded hills—mere whiffs of pale browns and yellows and greys right up to the skyline. But the winter woods can be sombre as well as fairylike. The next morning as I went up the drove road that leads to Minchmoor, I saw the sun sklenting obliquely through the trees in shafts of light which laid the woodman's track in tessellated greens and yellows. Pine trees at all times are solemn creatures. They always seem to be standing still, brooding in silence, dreaming dark dreams, in a world that is eerie and shadowy. Laughter and small talk may be all right among the fairy haunted birches—but in a dense pine wood you must creep silently lest you awake the dreamers from their age-long sleep.

On the other hand, the red osiers by the Bonnington Burn made a splash of brightness. But when summer comes there will be no such crimson blush on the osiers, for all their nakedness will be draped in the most delicate greenery.

This is just the most beautiful thing about the winter trees—their nakedness. Each tree stands up in all the distinction of its own personality. Indeed,

G

you never know the real character of a tree until you
see it stripped of all its leaves. The summer woods
are certainly very beautiful, but not half so beautiful
as the winter woods, when every branch is bare, and
you can see heaven through the tracery of a million
twigs. Walking in winter through a parkland that
is dotted with trees, you would never mistake a
gnarled oak for a stately elm, or an upright beech
for a spreading plane. As well mistake a hoary-
headed old gentleman with hands that are all knotted
and twisted with rheumatism for a graceful dandy
that looks down on every passer-by; or a clean-
limbed athlete for a stout fellow who has lost the
lissom figure of youth.

I have often wandered past Haystoun House in
spring, summer, and autumn when on my way up
Glensax. But as I came on this old, rambling, Scots
dwelling place, with its clean white face and its quaint
balcony, I stood in the silence of a February day and
gazed across the burn on a new wonder. The house
stands on an ivy-covered bank across the stream.
Immemorial trees screen it without hiding it. But
now, the snowdrops on the bank were like foaming
cascades falling right down to the water's edge. So
natural and so prodigal!

How many old policies in the Lothians and the
Borders at this moment are so thickly carpeted with
snowdrops that you feel as if you were walking
through fields of foam! Dalmeny, Arniston, Niddrie
Marischal, Dryburgh, Springwood Park. All down
Tweedside you can follow the gleam through the
trees by Rachan and Dawyck to Traquair.

XI

HERMITAGE CASTLE

A BORDER STRONGHOLD AND ITS STORY

A QUIET country house on the lower slopes of
Ruberslaw: a window wide open to the witcheries
of the summer night and the heavenly morning sun:
the scent of gardens with lawns and woods beyond:
and the waking dreams of a wandering man dispelled
by that most heartsome sound—the rhythmical
sweesh of a scythe in the luscious dew-drenched
grass. It was thus that the idyll of a midsummer day
and a long raid into Liddesdale began for us. Our
first thoughts on watching the masterly reaper
wielding his sharp scythe were of tall strong Border
reivers; old days and far rides to the castles and
keeps that lie tucked away in their bald security
among the glens and hills of Tweed and Ettrick,
Teviot and Liddel; Sir Walter's stravaigs with
Shortreed; and Queen Mary's record ride from
Jedworth to Hermitage and back again in one day.
But, if the Queen was able to ride fifty miles on a
wet October day over roadless hills and boggy
quagmires, surely we can manage the same distance
in comfort to-day in this year of grace, with the
sunshine all about us!

What a habble the historians have made over that same ride! George Buchanan and the Reformers setting her mad canter down to an outrageous lust for Bothwell; Andrew Lang and the later apologists for the mischancy Queen exalting her ten hours' journey into a noble jaunt on State affairs alone. But the facts at least are soon told.

James Hepburn, 4th Earl of Bothwell, her Keeper of the Marches, lay ill in the Castle of Hermitage, having been seriously wounded in the course of his duty as Warden of the Borders. Mary travelled down from Borthwick Castle to Jedburgh to hold a circuit court. Then, she set out on the 16th day of October 1566 to ride all the way to Hermitage and back, that she might see her wounded Warden and third husband-to-be. Whichever way she went, she would cross the moors from Jedburgh for her fifty miles' ride. Did she ride gaily up Rule Water? If so, she would climb the desolate heights of Earlside and dip down somewhere into Slitrig Water. Finally, she would reach Hermitage by way of Priesthaugh, Swire Knowe, and the Braidley Burn. On returning, her horse was bogged in what has ever since been called the Queen's Mire—a morass just south of Swire Knowe—where years ago a lady's spur of ancient pattern was found. It turned out a wet October day and the Queen reached Jedburgh soaked to the skin, tired out, and splashed to the eyes with mud. This cantrip cost her dear. For the adventurous Queen of Scots, who had known many sorrows, sins, and sicknesses in her short life, was next day laid up with a raging fever. For a week she hovered on the edge of death. On the ninth day

THE OLD BRIDGE, JEDBURGH

she grew perfectly cold and rigid. Moray had already his fingers on the Crown jewels. Claud Nau, her French secretary, tells us that mourning dresses were ordered and the funeral arrangements made. Even Bishop Leslie wrote from Jedburgh that " Her Majesty became deid and all her memberis cauld, her eine closit, mouth fast, and feit and armis stiff and cauld."

But Mary recovered, and M. le Croc, the French Ambassador, writing on 24th October, says that " in five or six days the Queen will be able to sign." Fifteen days after that, despite a relapse, she left Jedburgh for Craigmillar Castle, her healthiest home. But when we remember her sorry after-life, with the executioner's block at the hinder-end, can we wonder that Mary once sighed and said, " Would that I had died at Jedworth "?

We, too, take the old road up Rule Water, until we reach the high bare moors about Chapel o' Cross and Earlside. Up here on this perfect summer day, with sunshine sklenting out of a sky that hangs with clouds, the visibility is splendid. The Border landscape rolls away from Ruberslaw to the Eildons, with the dim blue line of the Lammermoors, the Moorfoots, and the Tweedside hills making a heartsome horizon. Then, passing down the Whitterhope Burn, a sharp turn to the right up the pleasant water of Hermitage, and we are standing in wonder opposite the Castle.

A great grey stronghold, hoary with antiquity, sleeping amid the silence and sunshine on the side of this whispering stream, like an old warrior tired out after seven centuries of battle—how the crimson

tides of war must have roared round these walls!
So, in a dream of history, we cross the Hermitage
Water by the wooden bridge and follow the path
across the turf to the narrow postern door. The
cows are browsing in the heat, and the place is as
still as death. Within the narrow courtyard we stand
in the deep shade and listen. Then the old-time
stories, like the winds of memory, come soughing
through our souls.

Somewhere, away back in the dim days of the early
centuries, a holy man must have set up his cell
at Hermitage. Then Walter de Bolbeck granted
" to God and St Mary and Brother William of
Mercherley " the hermitage beside this very water
which was then called the Merching Burn. Later
on, in the thirteenth century, Liddesdale was in the
hands of the De Soulis family, for a castle was built
here by Nicholas de Soulis, who lived in the reigns
of Alexander II. and Alexander III. In those days
the Border was defined in this district by Liddel
Water, and quite naturally Henry III. began to
think that this new-made stronghold was too much
of a menace to his English march. So in 1243 he
invaded Scotland, and thus began the great struggle
which for centuries raged round Hermitage.

How often the leasehold of this ancient keep
changed from family to family of fighting Scots.
From the great De Soulis to William de Douglas,
and from Douglas to the Earl of Angus in 1398.
Then came the Bold Buccleuchs, who were appointed
governors of the Castle in the same century (1470)
by the family of Angus. A hundred years later
Hermitage became the property of the Scotts of

Buccleuch, into whose hands it fell through their connection with Francis Stewart, Earl of Bothwell. The Duke of Buccleuch thoroughly repaired the Castle in 1821, and it is to him we owe its present splendid state of preservation.

The very oldest part of Hermitage is the innermost wall of the original keep. The stones are clean-cut, square-dressed Norman-like blocks. The oblong larger keep which was next erected round the oldest part was built in the fourteenth century, the ruder stonework giving ample proof of its later date. Then in the fifteenth century great square extensions or towers were erected at the four corners of the earlier Castle, with an arch at either end to carry the upper defence works. So Hermitage stands to-day a splendidly preserved Border castle of three periods, like three Chinese boxes, one inside the other. Within the Castle itself there are two wells, a stone boiler, and a circular stone oven, the remains of a finely built wheel stairway, and many other details which delight the antiquary and the architect.

But the place of darkest memories is the dungeon. Down in that murderous hole many a sorry prisoner of a Soulis or Douglas languished to death. But there was one famous victim of whom we have before us to-day a written life—Sir Alexander Ramsay of Dalwolsey, sometime Warden of the Middle Marches and Sheriff of Teviotdale. Sir William Douglas, the Knight of Liddesdale, was then the keeper of the Castle. Ramsay, his enemy, as Fordun tells us, " surpassed all others of his time in brave deeds and in bodily strength, whether in the field of battle or in the tournament." Douglas

by a trick of treachery seized Ramsay in 1342 while
he was holding his Court as Sheriff of Teviotdale in
the open church at Hawick, and having wounded the
Sheriff when he was in the act of offering a seat to
Douglas, the Keeper of Hermitage thus stained the
flower of his chivalry, and threw poor Ramsay into
the dungeon.   No food whatever was supplied to the
Sheriff, but tradition tells us that above the dungeon
there was a granary, and that Sir Alexander lived
for seventeen days on the grain that fell through the
chinks of the floor above him.   Then he died
miserably of starvation.   Five hundred years after,
a mason who was at work restoring the Castle came
upon the dungeon, and descending with a light into
the chamber of horrors found some bones, an old-
fashioned sword, and a bridle-bit of great antiquity,
also a quantity of husks of oats!   The bridle-bit was
given to Sir Walter Scott, who in turn gave it to
the ninth Earl of Dalhousie, one of Wellington's
generals and a distinguished soldier, like his ancestor,
Sir Alexander Ramsay.   The husks of oats?   Well,
that is another question, and our doubts are inflamed
the more as we stand above the gaping hole in the
floor and recognise that this chamber above was
undoubtedly a guard-room (not a granary), with a
shot-hole in the wall for the sentry.   And yet a
sympathetic sentry might easily himself have been
the granary, especially when the prisoner was the
bravest soldier in Scotland.

Coming out into the blazing heat again, we sit
down by Hermitage Water and have lunch beneath
a tree.   The water is of a lovely golden-green colour,
and in the still pools we can watch the lazy trout

nosing their way up-stream, or hear them plopping in the summer silence. Even this golden stream entered into the natural defences of the Castle, for Hermitage Water flows in front, and on either side of the stronghold a little stream still flows down to meet the larger one.

A hundred yards or so up the water stands the chapel of Hermitage. It is a place of ruined walls now, about fifty feet by twenty-five, eloquent, crying out of holy things forgot, appealing in its very desolations. The stones are all square dressed like those in the oldest part of the Castle. Inside the walls we stand and mark the three altar steps, the primitive font leaning against the south wall, the ancient ash tree growing monstrously through the vacancy where the west window once burned red in the sunset. Two buttresses would seem to indicate a little chancel arch. No carving or ornament marred the simplicity of these early chapels. Here is the arch of an early pointed window all cut out of one stone. Yonder are stone mullions with sinkings cut in them for the window glass. A rare litter of ancient stones, which would doubtless have been long ago removed but for the remoteness of Hermitage.

But most remarkable of all are the earthen defences of the chapel and the Castle, which may still be traced in the turf from the top of the little hill to the north. Yonder round the Castle are the mounds of defence and the surrounding ditches. A line of green-grown ramparts runs all the way from the Castle to this round mound on the hill where we stand, then down in a straight line past the chapel to the waterside, with a ditch and rampart round the

square of the churchyard itself. Hard-by the churchyard to the west lies a great rectangular rampart,
like a Roman camp divided into three oblong spaces.
Here may have stood many outbuildings. Another
round mound at the extremity by the waterside
completes the defences of this formidable stronghold.

And what of that grave-like mound between
Hermitage Water and the wall of the consecrated
God's-acre? Tradition says it is the Cout o'
Keilder's grave. For the Cout, who was of great
stature and desperate strength, came over from his
stronghold in Northumberland on a hunting expedition to the ground of his greatest enemy, the wizard
de Soulis of Hermitage. John Leyden tells us in his
" Cout o' Keilder " that the great man's wife warned
him not to go.

> Gin you will ride on the Scottish side
>   Sore must thy Margaret mourn,
> For Soulis abhorr'd is Lydalls' lord,
>   And I fear you'll ne'er return.

But, then as now, the wilful man must have his
way, and the Cout was soon hacking a bloody lane
through the ranks of Soulis on Hermitage Water.
He was fey with slaughtering, and was just getting
near his arch-enemy, when he was overwhelmed by
numbers and received a wound. They drove him
then into the water, where, encumbered by his heavy
armour, he fought and fell like a stag at bay. Up
again he got on his feet, but they pushed him down
again and again. Oh brave Cout, what of thy
Margaret's words now? For just then Soulis and his
men actually held him down in the water until he

was drowned like a ratten under a bank. Then they buried him outside the pale of holy church, under this grassy mound, unoriented and unblessed. Thus the great Cout (chief) o' Keilder perished. Standing here on the green howe, we rub our chins in doubt again—for, when this mound was opened years ago, no herculean bones were found. Oh, horrid battle of Romance and Fact—how we hate the reasonable issue! But, even while our cool heads accept the Fact, our hot hearts, inflamed by old songs and ancient chivalries, cling to the Romance.

The seven or eight miles from Hermitage to Ewes Water and the Mosspaul Burn are unrivalled in the borderland for lonely grandeur. These high hills and wild cleuchs, with their gashes and burn courses, must have been fell reiving regions long ago. The men fought, the women wept, and the little bairns ran fatherless on the braes. You can hear the bridle-bits jingling, the horses galloping, the swords clashing on breastplate and helm, while the bugle sounds adown the dale. Caerlanrig, Teviothead, Branxholm Tower, and Goldielands—how the old life and romance of the Border sings in the soul as we sweep down Teviotdale!

And then, as we creep past the little thatched cottage of John Leyden in Denholm village—that scholarly pundit and understudy of the great Sir Walter—the sun is setting in all its glory and we climb the steps of Spital Tower and look out of the open windows on the new-made hay, that lies so sweet and fragrant now, in the evening light beyond the lawn.

XII

IN THE LAP OF THE LOWTHERS

THE COUNTRY OF THE COVENANT

It was a day of beauty—blue, windless and warm—when we made our way down the Dalveen Pass. We sat on the heather near a grave at Troloss, with the Mayday sun beaking down on us in the silence of noon, until the solemn green sheephills became instinct with memories of the long ago, when here in Dalveen and over yonder in Enterkin the Covenanters were hunted by Bloody Clavers and his troopers. The only thing that outmatched the external glories of the day was the inner sough of the Covenant that kept sounding through the heart, like a wandering wind with a wail in it. The lonely cry of a whaup above Comb Head; the grave over yonder on the next knoll; with the thought of Durisdeer and Kirkbride, those twin kirkyards of incomparable memories—these things sent a surge of old-time sentiments through the soul, and with a mysterious suddenness on this day of shimmering beauty a mist began to gather on the face of Comb Head where no mist was.

Durisdeer was our first trysting-place, but it was still a long step down the Carron Water out of this stey glenhead into the rich pasturelands that lie below the mill.

HERMITAGE CASTLE

Yonder it is at last—the kirkyard of our dreams! A square grey tower rises above a clump of trees, and a handful of houses clusters round the ancient shrine of St Cuthbert. A hot silence lies over the kirk, the cottages, and the graves, as we pass in at the iron gate. Here surely is a place that has been well beloved of the country folk, both gentle and simple; for the dead lie crowded together and well happit.

Out-by—the kirk, like a cross, stands grey and austere, with its tower against the sky, and the great trees all around to shelter both the living and the dead from the ill winds of the world. Beyond the trees lie the round green hills; these homely arms of earth, our mother. A touch of heather here, and a deep red scaur yonder, like a bloodstained gash in the green—and far away to the south-west beyond the lands of Nith, a shimmering line of dim hills again, from Cairnkinna to Tynrondoon, ethereal, heavenly, pure. Such is this old kirkyard of Durisdeer which lies like a tale of life that is told, in a lap of the Lowthers.

What wild inclemencies and wintry winds must sometimes blow about the kirk itself! What dazzling drift must cover the graves, when the snow smoors up the old square door! But now, in the warm afternoon, the murmur of the kirk burn near-by and the hum of insects in the trees make the only sounds.

Up there, above the door, is an ancient sundial that has marked time for many generations, and its date, 1699, leaves us in no doubt as to the age of the kirk. Here lies the tomb of Daniel M'Michael, brother to James, the Black M'Michael, who him-

self shot the curate of Carsphairn. It was this same
Daniel who was afterwards shot up at Dalveen for
his adherence to the Covenanted Faith.

Read the names on the headstones, and the
romance of many a bein farm town and shepherd's
cottage comes over the mind like the lilt of an old
song. Chanlockfoot, Glenmanna, Camplebridge,
Drumereuil, Hapland, Humbiehome, and Kirkbride! They are all there, and to whisper them
over is to feel that grip at the heart which means
so much to a Lowland Scot.

Inside the kirk we step softly. Here is the great
mausoleum of the Queensberrys, with its ancient
marble tomb and its four-pillared marble canopy
brought from Rome. In Durisdeer the great James
Douglas (1622-1711), 2nd Duke of Queensberry,
and his Duchess, with many another of his noble
house, lie side by side with their own shepherds from
the hills. For when it comes to the hinmost sleep
we lay aside all our differences and lie together
in the same bed, the green grass our only covering.

Here on the window-sill lie two ancient wrought-
iron relics—the brackets for the preacher's hour-
glass, and the baptismal bowl. These things are all
rust-eaten and derelict now—but the sight of them
calls up pictures of the past. How many in days
gone by must have watched with wearied eyes the
preacher's hand turning the sand-glass when the
sermon was long! The same hand sprinkled the
water from the bowl on the little ones' faces!

The pulpit of Durisdeer stands with its back to
the tomb of the Queensberrys, separated only by a

great glass screen. Its plain deal boards, the square pews with a little table in the centre of each, the ample galleries and the austere walls—it is all here as it has ever been in our ancient country kirks. In the vestry hangs a Roll of Honour, that sign of our own times' sacrifice. Again the old fight for freedom, and Daniel M'Michael out-by is kin to some whose names are hanging there in the vestry to-day.

But when we enter the most ancient part of the old kirk of Durisdeer we see in the dim light enormous walls, stone fireplaces, built-up windows, and great oaken beams fastened with wooden pins, all of which call up visions of monks and lay brothers at meat in the refectory, or reading missals round the winter fires. For as far back as 1570 the kirk of St Cuthbert at Durisdeer was served from the Cathedral of St Mungo. The old tortuous stair to the tower, the rotting beams, the beedle's bell-rope ready for his hand as he enters this ancient place of memories to sound a summons for God's folk to come and pray—it is all a mingling of the old and the new, the dead and the living, the present and the past.

Outside in the sunshine sitting by M'Michael's grave, we see the whole tragic story played over again. There had been a handful of the M'Michael band surprised by fifty soldiers who found them sleeping in a shieling in Morton parish. All the men of the Covenant escaped except Daniel M'Michael, who was ailing. The soldiers, who were commanded by John Dalziel, son of Sir Robert Dalziel of Kirk-michael—as the tombstone tells—wounded poor M'Michael while taking him, and carried him off

that night to the kirk of Durisdeer. Did he spend
the night in that same old part of the kirk where we
have just seen the old beams and the ample fireplaces? For it was mid-winter, and doubtless the
logs blazed on the open hearth, as the soldiers sat
warming themselves just as the monks had done in
ages past. The captain tried to force M'Michael's
tongue, but his prisoner would say nothing to hurt
his friends. Then, death as a threat was shaken in
his face.

" Do you not know that your life is in my hand? "
cried Dalziel.

" No, sir; I know my life is in the Lord's hand,
and if He see good, He can make you the instrument
to take it away."

Then he was told he must die on the morrow.

That night he enjoyed a time of such communion
with God that some of the rough troopers envied
his tranquillity and were pricked in their own
consciences.

Next day, the 31st of January 1685, the soldiers
made for Enterkin Pass with Daniel M'Michael—
that gloomy way of death up which the frightened
country folks were accustomed to drag local suicides
on sledges to bury them on the no-man's-land of the
Lowthers where three lairds' properties met. But
on this January day the pass was so full of drifted
snow that Dalziel had to turn aside. He took his
prisoner over to John Hoatson's farm at Nether
Dalveen, and there they halted for fear of an
ambuscade.

Liberty was granted to Daniel M'Michael to pray.
While he prayed aloud the soldiers were filled with

wonder at the outgait of his petitions.   Then he sang part of the 42nd Psalm: —

> O why art thou cast down, my soul,
> Why thus with grief opprest?

He read the sixteenth chapter of St John: —

> A little while, and ye shall not see me . . . in the world ye shall have tribulation : but be of good cheer; I have overcome the world.

Sitting here by his grave to-day we can almost hear the reading, the singing and the prayer.   But there comes another sound—sharp, quick, familiar. For at the crack of four muskets Daniel M'Michael lay dead on the snow-white fields of the dark Dalveen.

And this old ash tree by the grave?   It was planted by Prophet Peden's own hand in remembrance of his old friend.   It has burst once more into greenery, and we touch it with reverence today; for, sitting in the silence and the sunshine, we know that its fresh, new leaves are a symbol of Eternal Life.   This martyr of the Covenant, all who have died in the flat lands across the Channel seas, the Roll of Honour in the Durisdeer vestry, stand for the same thing through all the centuries, wherever men live and fight and die for faith and freedom.

And ere we leave this old kirkyard of Durisdeer, there is one more song which we hear and sometimes sing.   It was written by Lady John Scott who kept tryst with her beloved in this same quiet place of graves.   We too know the tryst word, and have come to-day to keep our tryst here.

H

We'll meet nae mair at sunset, when the weary day is
    dune,
Nor wander hame thegither, by the lee licht o' the
    mune!
I'll hear your step nae langer, amang the dewy corn,
For we'll meet nae mair my bonniest, either at eve or
    morn.

The yellow broom is waving abune the sunny brae,
And the rowan berries dancing, where the sparkling
    waters play.
Tho' a' is bright and bonnie, it's an eerie place to me,
For we'll meet nae mair, my dearest, either by burn or
    tree.

Far up into the wild hills, there's a kirkyard auld and
    still,
Where the frosts lie ilka morning, and the mists hang
    low and chill.
And there ye sleep in silence, while I wander here my
    lane,
Till we meet ance mair in heaven, never to part again.

.   .   .   .

The next time I took the road through the
Lowthers it was a midsummer day. I was making
for the lonely little ruin of Kirkbride Church, which
stands on a green hill, five or six miles from
Sanquhar.

It is a very modest ruin, only forty-two feet long
by fourteen wide, with the remains of a tiny chapel
opening into the Church through a rounded arch on
the north side. The greater part of one gable still
remains. But, except for part of a door or window
here and there, Kirkbride to-day is just a rickle of
stones.

And yet—this lonely spot has inspired the finest Covenanting poem which has ever been written, for the holy fame of Kirkbride rests on the fact that many Covenanters were buried there. It is sometimes futile to recommend pilgrimages to such spots, for when it comes to ruined walls or a grave, the eye and heart can only see what they bring the power to see. There are, however, some whose feet delight to travel over hills and heather to seek out a Covenanting shrine or brood over a martyr stone. It is for all such that I set down this record of the moorland poet who has immortalized Kirkbride.

To reach Kirkbride you cross the Dalveen Pass by Durisdeer. Then, you take the north road up the Nith as far as Enterkinfoot. Here, a poor side road strikes off to the right under the railway, and slews left up the little valley of the Ha' Cleuch for a mile, until you come to a steep turn over a bridge. From this spot you climb up a steep hill to the south, past Kirkbride Farm, and beyond that to the top of the green hill. There, you will find the ruins of Kirkbride, standing between the valley of the Nith and the little glen of Ha' Cleuch.

There is a far view to the south-west from Kirkbride. The blue hills roll away in a dim procession—Dunduff, Cairnkinna, Countam. Yonder on the horizon are the wild Galloway fastnesses, beyond the valleys of the Scaur, Shinnel and Walwhat. About your feet, there is nothing but a green sheep walk, with the ewes nibbling the grass in the silence of the summer noon, a grave or two, and the grey walls of the old kirk. A breath of air soughs about this place of graves to temper the heat, and immediately you think of the Eternal Spirit brooding over man's mortality.

With great reluctance we left Kirkbride and once more took the Sanquhar road northwards as far as Mennock. Then began the long steep ascent of the Mennock Pass to the village of Wanlockhead. Again I had a tryst to keep at Wanlockhead, for there, men and women had gathered from far and near to be present at the unveiling of a tablet on the wall of the old school to the memory of Robert Reid (Rob. Wanlock), author of " Kirkbride," a great lover of this grey glen and the dwellers in it.

Wanlockhead and Leadhills claim to be the highest villages in Scotland, for the road between them is just a trifle over 1400 feet. These twin villages are tucked away among the quiet glens of the Lowther Hills, each of them high set like the eyrie of an eagle. Lead was worked in Glengonnar Water as early as 1239, and indeed the Romans may have worked it here. The Lead Mines, however, were little known until 1512, and these, alas, have within recent years been closed down. Not only lead, but silver and gold were found in olden times in the four burns of Glengonar, Short Cleuch, Mennock and Wanlock, which were called the Four Rivers of Eden. Indeed, the " bonnet pieces " of James V. of Scotland were all made of gold found at Wanlockhead. A " bonnet piece " was a gold coin of the time of James V., so called because the king was represented on it as wearing a bonnet, and not a crown. These " bonnet pieces " were the most beautiful coins in the Scots series, and Ruddiman wrote in 1739 in the Introduction to *Diplomata et Numismata Scotiæ*,

" Certainly, the gold pieces of that prince, commonly called *bonnet pieces*, are so remarkable, not only for their compactness, but for the art of engraving, that I do not know if there was ever any coin, either then or at present, in all Europe, that comes nearer to the Roman coin in elegance."

Is it to be wondered at, then, that the whole of this gold bearing district in the Lowther Hills was called in olden days God's Treasure House in Scotland? I have a friend whose wedding ring is made of Wanlockhead gold. Indeed, Queen Mary herself wears a ring to-day made of gold gathered here.

Many hardy men and women of the Covenant and more than one Scots poem came from this neighbourhood. Allan Ramsay was born at Leadhills. James Hyslop, author of " The Cameronian's Dream," and Alexander Anderson, the " Surfaceman " poet, came from the parish of Kirkconnel close by. Also, in the graveyard of Leadhills I came on a tombstone with this almost incredible inscription: " John Taylor, died 137 years of age." Taylor is said to have worked as a lead miner for over a hundred years— surely an unbeatable record!

So this world on the heights bred not only stern Covenanters, but long livers and Scots poets. Because of its golden hearts as well as its gold-bearing burns, it might well be called God's Treasure House in Scotland.

Robert Reid was born in Wanlockhead on the 8th day of June 1850. The details of his life are soon told. He was educated in the village school, went to an office in Glasgow when he was fifteen, was thereafter in Belfast for a time, and finally emigrated to Montreal, where he entered the firm of Henry Morgan & Co. He remained in Canada for thirty years, and died on 1st June 1922, in his seventy-second year.

My first introduction to the poetry of this bard of the moorlands was through reading in Sir William Robertson Nicoll's " Songs of Rest " the poem which has given Robert Reid immortal fame—" Kilbride." It is a ballad of the purest sentiment wrung from the Covenanting heart of Scotland. If poetry means seeing the infinite in things, then Robert Reid was a true poet. He saw beauty in the ordinaries of life. He touched the heart of every Scot by singing in his native tongue. Moreover, he struck certain universal notes which will appeal to men and women in every age.

The first note is the love of country which begets in the heart a perpetual longing for home.

Never could this man of the moors forget those sonsy, round-topped hills: this green-set village; the wide moorlands over which the caller winds are for ever blowing; the music of the whaups and peewees in spring; the wimple of the summer burns; or the old kindly faces which appeared again and again to him, like ghosts of home, flitting across three thousand leagues of sea. His poems are full of an exile's longings. Nowhere is this more apparent than in his incomparable poem " The Whaup ": —

> Fu' sweet is the lilt o' the laverock
>   Frae the rim o' the clud at morn;
> The merle pipes weel in his mid-day biel'
>   In the heart o' the bendin' thorn;

The blythe bauld sang o' the mavis
   Rings clear in the gloamin' shaw;
But, the whaup's wild cry in the gurly sky
   O' the moorlan' dings them a'.

For, what's in the lilt o' the laverock
   Tae touch ought mair than the ear?
The merle's lown craik in the tangled brake
   Can start nae memories dear:
And even the sang o' the mavis
   But waukens a love dream tame
Tae the whaup's wild cry on the breeze blawn by,
   Like a wanderin' word frae hame.

What thochts o' the lang grey moorlan'
   Start up when I hear that cry!
The times we lay on the heathery brae
   At the well lang syne gane dry:
And aye as we spak' o' the ferlies
   That happened afore-time there,
The whaup's lane cry on the win' cam' by
   Like a wild thing tint in the air.

And though I hae seen mair ferlies
   Than grew in the fancy then,
And the gowden gleam of the boyish dream
   Has slipped frae my soberer brain,
Yet—even yet—if I wander
   Alane by the moorlan' hill,
That queer wild cry frae the gurly sky
   Can tirl my heart strings still.

His second note is that of human love. For no poet ever left love out. Rob Wanlock knew right well that those who love most, suffer most. You have only to read his "May Moril" to realize how deeply the poet understood the bitter pathos of a lost love:—

O hooly and wae I laid her doon
                In her hinmaist rest,
And back i' the glen I lookit roun'
                At oor herrit nest;
And bare, bare noo were the muirlan's grey
                Where the licht o' her love gart a' things shine,
And I saw that nocht i' the warld wad be
The same as it was to my joyfu' ee,
                When we wadit the brackens knee by knee,
And sweet May Moril was hale and mine.
The brier rose blooms on the open shaw,
                As it did lang syne,
And the milk-white blossom hings on the haw
                I' the warm sunshine.
But blossom and bud hae tint their charms,
                They may rot where they gather and fa, for me,
And O', gin I hadna a thocht tae rise
Tae sweet May Moril ayont the skies,
Where my heart baith e'enin' and mornin' lies,
                Hoo sad wad the lang grey moorlan' be!

But, the deepest note in Rob Wanlock's poems is
that of religion.   He was born in the Country of the
Covenant, where to-day the Martyr Stones stand
four-square on many a wind-swept moor and in many
a quiet kirkyard.   They bear silent witness to the
brave men and women who in their day and
generation gave their lives for a faith which they
valued more than anything that this world can yield.
In the poet's veins ran the blood of the martyrs.

I never read Dr John Brown's " Enterkin "
without thinking of Daniel MacMichael's brother
James—the Black MacMichael, as he was called. He
was the fowler to the laird of Maxwelton, and the
leader of the Covenanting party which lay ambus-
caded above the Enterkin Pass to rescue a number of

prisoners who were being convoyed to Edinburgh by the dragoons. The soldiers had reached the narrowest part of the defile when they were challenged from the heights to give up the prisoners. The refusal was accompanied by a dragoon's oath. The fowler raised his gun. Sergeant Kelt rolled from his horse with a bullet through his head. The dead man rolled down the steep slope of the gorge into the stream, and the place is called after him to this day. On a later occasion the Black MacMichael engaged Claverhouse himself in a hand to hand fight, and the fowler of Maxwelton would have slain Bloody Clavers had not a dragoon rode up from behind and cleft his skull in two. MacMichael was buried in Kirkbride, as his brother was buried in Durisdeer.

In his poem of " Kirkbride " Rob Wanlock conjures up the dreams of a dying Covenanter who has been through the ordeal of the Killing Times. We can almost hear the mutterings of this aged hero of the Covenant as he recalls the past in that ecstatic moment of illumination which so often comes to those who are just on the verge of eternity. The winsome face of his beloved, and the unforgettable sound of her singing. The notes of a psalm wafted down the glen on the fitful wind where the huddled flock of Christ is worshipping God. The voice of the Black MacMichael, his old comrade in arms, whose broad sword did great things for the Lord. The groping of the feeble fingers, as this dying shepherd makes a last effort to get at his crook and plaid, ere he sets out on his hinmost journey. His instinctive call for the Holy Book with its well-thumbed pages of comfort and hope. The Cample Ford, known to him

from boyhood, which has now become to this stern
campaigner of Christ a homely symbol for the
crossing of Jordan.   Then, the last sad act of brotherhood, when his friends carry his old done body up
the steep brae to green Kirkbride, where he will rest
in peace till the trumpet sounds *reveille!* It is all
there in the poem.   The love, the faith, the conscience, the eternal certitude which has been the very
marrow of Scots life and religion.

Robert Burns wrote " The Cottar's Saturday
Night " after hearing the holy phrase, " Let us
worship God," from the lips of his father when he
was about to open the Book at his own kitchen
fireside.   So also did Robert Wanlock Reid write
" Kirkbride," when he remembered that an old native
of his own countryside made this dying request: —
" Bury me in Kirkbride, for much of God's redeemed
dust lies there."

The best memorial of any man is his work.   So
the most lasting shrine of this moorland singer will
be found by generations yet unborn in those unforgettable verses: —

Bury me in Kirkbride,
   Where the Lord's redeemed anes lie ;
The auld kirkyard on the green hillside
     Under the open sky—
     Under the open sky,
On the briest o' the brae sae steep,
   And side by side wi' the banes that lie
Streikit there in their hinmost sleep.
   This puir dune body maun sune be dust,
     But it thrills wi' a stound o' pride
To ken it will mix wi' the great and just
     That are buried in thee, Kirkbride.

Wheesht! Did the saft wind speak?
 Or a yammerin' nicht bird cry?
Did I dream that a warm hand touched my cheek,
     And a winsome face gaed by—
     And a winsome face gaed by?
Wi' a far aff licht in its e'en—
 A licht that bude come frae the dazzlin' sky,
For it spak' o' the sternies sheen.
     Age may be donnert and dazed and blin',
       But I'll warrant whate'er betide,
     A true heart there made tryst wi' my ain,
       And the tryst word was—Kirkbride!

Hark! Frae the far hilltaps,
 And laich frae the lanesome glen,
A sweet psalm tune, like a late dew, draps
     Its wild notes doon the wind—
     Its wild notes doon the wind,
Wi' a kent soun' ower my mind,
 For we sang 't on the muir, a wheen huntit men,
Wi' our lives in our hand lang syne.
     But, naething on earth can disturb this sang,
       Were it Clavers in a' his pride,
     For it's raised by the Lord's ain ransomed thrang
       Foregathered abune Kirkbride.

I hear May Moril's tongue
 That I wistna to hear again,
And there 'twas the Black MacMichael's sang
     Clear in the closin' strain—
     Clear in the closin' strain,
Frae his big heart bauld and true;
 It stirs my soul as in days bygane
When his gude braidsword he drew:
 I needs must be aff to the moors ance mair,
     For he'll miss me by his side;
 In the thrang o' the battle I aye was there,
     And sae maun it be in Kirkbride.

Rax me my staff and plaid,
   That in readiness I may be,
And dinna forget that *The Book* be laid
      Open across my knee—
      Open across my knee,
And a text close by my thoom;
   And tell me true, for I scarce can see
That the words are " Lo I come ! "
      Then carry me through at the Cample Ford,
         And up the lang hillside;
      And I'll wait for the comin' o' God the Lord
         In a neuk o' the auld Kirkbride.

XIII

EAST LOTHIAN

THE GARDEN OF SCOTLAND

I

Blessed be the man who lights the fire on his first
hearthstone within a morning's walk of Lammerlaw,
or sets out on the great adventure of life and love
beneath the shadow of Soutra. Then will the
Lammermoors for ever be to him the Hills of Home.
Although he may travel wide and far, his heart will
keep turning to that eastland country where the
winds blow caller from the cleuchs. The landscape,
whose northern bounds is the restless sea and whose
southern boundary is the heather, falls away from
the edge of the moors in billows of green fields and
corn-lands to meet the North Sea that breaks on the
rocks and yellow sands which mark the coast of the
Shire of Haddington.

Standing by the Watering Stone on Soutra, you
can sweep in with the eye the whole of this garden
of Scotland—from the Pentlands to the Bass and
the dim blue waters of the Forth with the Fife lands
beyond; and—if the day be a snell one in spring,
with a touch of north wind to clear your vision—
far furth the Forth to the cloud-like Braes of Angus.
At night the darkness is lit most wondrously by
those stars of the sea which wink out safety to the

mariner—Inchkeith, one long flash; Fidra, two flashes; the May Isle, four; and the Bass, six. In all this land, there is nothing rugged or wild, like the scenery of the Highlands. The hills are round, and restful. The laigh lands are rich beyond a crofter's dreams, with the very finest of wheat and corn and sheep. Dotted over the rolling champaign are shrines of history, and old ancestral halls whose names are linked with the best blood in Scotland.

A man of sentiment may be excused if he traces with a loving eye the rough bounds of the county on which he gazed daily, from the windows of his first home. East Lothian thrusts its seaboard northwards in a great semicircle of rocks and sandy dunes and grassy links, from Prestonpans to the Dunglass Burn, near Cockburnspath. The boundary line creeps up from the Forth, past the old Tower of Elphingstone and the kirk of Ormiston, following the Linndean Water to Lowrie's Den on Soutra Hill. Then, it wanders eastward over Ninecairn Edge to Lammerlaw, takes in the Kilpallet Heights and just touches the Fasney Water. It continues east by St Agnes and makes a little thrust down to Cranshaws Kirk on the Whiteadder. Finally it swings round Monynut Edge and across the head-waters of the Eye, until, following the Berwick Burn and the Dunglass Burn, it loses itself in the sea below Bilsdean.

Like Gaul of old, East Lothian is divided into three parts—the Hill Parishes in the lonely Lammermoors; the Central Parishes of the plain, which run for twenty miles from Tranent to Dunbar; and the Seaboard Parishes which encircle the coast from

Prestonpans to Cockburnspath. So there are three distinct tribes in the county—the sheepfolk of the Lammermoors; the farming folk who live on the rich lands that lie on both sides of the River Tyne; and the golfing folk who swarm along the coast line in summer, and play the ancient game on the finest chain of sea-links in Scotland. The Tyne Water begins as a mere driblet of a burn near the old inn on Middleton Moor and dissects the county from end to end, flowing into the sea near St Baldred's Cradle in Belhaven Bay.

It takes an intelligent tramp years to know East Lothian and a whole lifetime is not long enough to love it. Who would not linger on a warm September day in the old-world villages of Gifford, Garvald, Stenton, and Spott, each with a sleepy atmosphere all its own. Spott is the most notorious of all, because here on Sunday, 24th September 1570, Rev. John Kello the parson of Spott strangled his wife in the manse and immediately went into the church and preached to his people as if nothing had happened! There are lonely spots like Pressmennan Loch, or the Hill Road near Priestlaw, where you may light your fire and count on solitude for a companion. But those who have ettlings after a day or two of crowded pleasure, have only to foregather at Levenhall and follow me along the high road to Haddington and they will see this land of plenty stretching away on every side.

Great men of history meet us, one by one, like daylight ghosts as we travel towards Haddington. Already we have passed Pinkie with a painful twist in the heart, for there in 1547 that great Englishman

Somerset, thrashed us, in a vain attempt to make
us break the Auld Alliance with France. In that
little ruined Tower of Dolphinton tradition still
has it that Cromwell once stayed. But surely the
ghost of an ill-used wife still flits about old Preston-
grange House down yonder! Till 1770 it was the
home of that notorious Lord of Session, Lord
Grange, who was outwardly a very pious presbyterian, but inwardly an unscrupulous political
schemer. It is an ill thing for any man to judge
between another man and his wife. But, even in
those old days, surely a wife had her rights! Whatever, therefore, may have been the truth of the
rumours about the lady, Lord Grange the pious
lawyer determined to get rid of her. So, one day
in 1732, he calmly announced that my Lady Grange
had died suddenly. The countryside condoled with
him and there was a solemn funeral, with my Lord
sniffling like a hypocrite in crepe and weepers behind
the hearse. But, while the earth was thudding down
on the empty coffin in the grave, the sorrowing
husband was wondering how his hired thieves, the
Highland rascals, were getting on. They had gagged
and kidnapped the poor lady in Edinburgh, carried
her off first to the Lowlands, then to that wild Vale
of Weeping, Glencoe, and finally to the shores of
Loch Hourn, which to this day is called the Loch
of Hell. From that mischancy region they shipped
her to the loneliest rock off the Outer Hebrides—
St Kilda. There she lived for years. No provisions
were sent to her. She was entirely dependent on the
kindness of the local minister. In 1740 a letter
written by her reached the Lord Advocate, and she

was removed, first to Assynt, and later on to Skye. She died there in the year of the great rebellion, 1745, and was buried in Trumpan Kirkyard. During the investigations which followed, that pious rascal, her husband, pursed his lips in injured innocence, and falling back on man's oldest excuse, he blamed the woman. But the real reason of his action probably was, that he wished to prevent the poor lady from revealing his own Jacobite intrigues. An old story now, but it is nailed to the door of Preston Grange.

There is another sough of the Forty-five near Prestonpans station, for it was there that Bonnie Prince Charlie gained his nameliest victory over that late riser, Sir John Cope. It was largely owing to the help of young Anderson of Whitburgh that the Jacobites defeated the English, for he pointed out the only safe way through a local swamp. This enabled the Highlanders to surprise Cope's army by a night manœuvre. So, the dawn saw the clean heels of Cope's chargers galloping eastward, and the victorious Highlanders gathering loot to their hearts' content. Only one heroic figure stood out in Cope's army—Colonel Gardiner, a true soldier and a Christian gentleman, whose house of Bankton you can see, and whose birthplace you will find commemorated by a tablet let into the garden wall of the old house of Burnfoot, near Carriden, twenty-five miles further up the Forth. In the mêlée he bravely stood his ground encouraging his men, until he fell mortally wounded.

Further along our road the old Collegiate Church and Castle of Seton remind us that Queen Mary was a frequent visitor in these parts. Indeed, just two

I

days after the murder of Darnley she arrived here on a Sunday with Bothwell. She won an archery match with him against Seton and Huntly, and the losers afterwards entertained the Queen and Bothwell to dinner in an inn at Tranent.

At Tranent coal was first worked in Scotland. In a chartulary of Newbattle Abbey there is a charter of Seyer de Quincey about the year 1210, granting to the monks of Newbattle *Insuper carbonarium in territoria de Travernent*. At the battle of Pinkie in 1547 the folks of Tranent hid in the workings, but the English lighted fires at the entrances and suffocated them. Until the year 1775 coal-miners were practically serfs or indentured criminals, and were sold or transferred along with the pit in which they worked. The men dug the coal, while the women hauled it in wheel-less hutches, creeping on hands and knees, harnessed to the hutch. They also carried it in baskets on their back up long ladders or spiral staircases to the surface. As punishment for slight faults the miners were sometimes yoked in iron collars and made to draw gins, under the lash of a whip, or they were tied behind a horse and forced to go backwards all day. Memories are long, and this old sad story has left its mark to-day. When the pendulum of history swings, who can tell how far it will go in the other direction?

To the south of Tranent, the Tower of Elphinstone can be seen—an old fifteenth-century Scots keep, with walls twelve feet thick which are honeycombed with secret rooms. Here George Wishart was brought from Ormiston Hall to face Cardinal Beaton. A certain young man called John Knox, who was tutor to the boys at Longniddry House, wished to go with him. But Wishart said: " Nay— return to your bairns, and God bless you. One is sufficient for a sacrifice." Not long afterwards Beaton looked out of his window at St Andrews and saw Wishart burning in the faggot fires. But time is a whirligig, and soon we see the Cardinal's dead body hanging over the battlements on his own castle at St Andrews—an example of the old sad law of revenge which is older than history.

But, nothing taigles a tramp on his day's journey worse (or better) than old stories, old houses, and these day-lights ghosts of history.

The road now leads us through the little village of Gladsmuir—the moor of the gled or hawk. Here, in the old manse, lived Robertson the historian, who afterwards became the Principal of Edinburgh University. In Gladsmuir also, George Heriot, or " Jingling Geordie," spent his early days—that truly thrifty Scots Goldsmith, who followed James VI. to London, and combined moneylending and jewel selling to the Queen and courtiers so successfully, that he amassed a fortune, and left £23,000 to build the hospital which is one of the glories of Auld Reekie to-day.

This road runs practically on the broad backbone of East Lothian. A few miles more, and we are at the entrance to one of the most delightsome county towns in Scotland.

Haddington always reminds me of an old man dozing in the heat of a summer garden. The town sleeps to-day in the sunshine, lown and quiet, as if no storms of history had ever roared through its streets. Set, like a gem in the hollow of rich lands and orchards, with luscious fruits ripening on old walls, this ancient burgh has all the amenities of a rural metropolis—a slow running river, an old parish church, quaint streets, a weekly market, antique buildings and cloistered suburbs with dignified houses dreaming amid old-fashioned gardens. Through mists of blue-grey beauty the waters of the sluggish stream reflect the red tiles and crumbling walls of houses that are centuries old.

Haddington was a royal burgh in the time of David I. William the Lion sometimes stayed here. Alexander II. was born in the palace. But from century to century the town was sorely mishandled. The English burned it again and again. They beseiged it, harassed it, occupied it. King John, Edward IV., Hotspur, Hertford, Cromwell—they all set the torch to Haddington or in some way sent war roaring through its streets. But, since the day that Johnny Cope clattered through it from Preston-pans in 1745, the old town has slept in peace. So Haddington is like an old veteran of war, dovering quietly in his chair among the flowers and fruits of the monks' garden, the fight all gone out of him, as if he had never swung a broad-sword and cried "Come on!" Yet Johnstoun, in one of his seventeenth century epigrams, gave Haddington its true character when he wrote:—

Next unto Berwick, Haddington faced all
The greatest dangers, and was Scotland's wall.

A famous Abbey was founded here in 1178 by Ada, Countess of Northumberland, widow of Prince

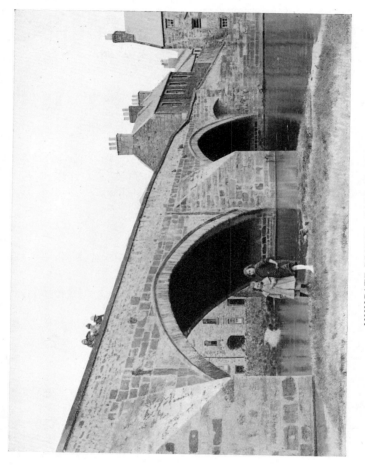

NUNGATE BRIDGE, HADDINGTON

Henry, the son of David I., and the mother of Malcolm IV. and William the Lion. But the monastery, which stood further down the river than the present church, has in the course of many burnings disappeared. It was this beautiful church, and not the present Parish Church of St Mary, that John Major called *Lampas Laudonide*, and that became so widely known as the Lamp of Lothian.

When in Haddington I am never tempted to dwell so much on the many details of its chequered history, as on the great men who lived there. There is something very bald about stone cut records like the one you will find on a house near the High Street, to this effect: —

> On the Fourth Day of October 1775, the River Tyne at three o'clock afternoon rose to this plate—
> "Quod non noctu deo gratias nemo enim periit."

I would rather see some proof that John Knox was born in Haddington, for that siccar man of faith is said to have acted as a notary within its walls from 1540 to 1543.

But in all my tramps through Haddington, I never fail to visit three places.

The first is the Kirkyard of St Mary's. There within the ruined choir can be seen the tombs of Chancellor Maitland of Lethington, brother of Queen Mary's secretary; the Duke of Lauderdale of evil fame; and Jane Welsh, the wife of Thomas Carlyle. Dean Ramsay tells us that Williamson, the Duke of Buccleuch's huntsman, was returning home one afternoon from the chase, and as he passed this same old kirk he saw an old woman holding the

grating in front of the Lauderdale Tomb, girning
and dancing with rage as she looked through. " Eh,
gudewife," said Williamson, " what ails ye? " " It's
the Duke o' Lauderdale!" screamed she of the
covenanting sympathies; " Eh, if I could only win
at him, I wad rax the banes o' him."

But it is the thought of Jane Welsh that haunts
us in Haddington. This bright genius of a woman
was linked in wedlock with that gruff philosopher
and man of letters, Thomas Carlyle. For forty
years he tried the patience of his brilliant sharp-
tongued wife—the little Mocking Bird as she was
called—who had, on her own confession, married
from ambition. True, he loved her all the time, in
his own silent, bear-like way. Then, after she was
gone, the old man, full of regrets, came creeping
into this ruined choir in the twilight, like a shadow
of himself, and kissed the tombstone on which he
wrote the most pathetic tribute of love that any man
ever carved on his wife's tomb: —

> In her bright existence she had more sorrows
> than are common, but also a soft invincibility, a
> capacity of discernment, and a noble loyalty of
> heart which are rare. For forty years she was
> the true and loving helpmate of her husband,
> and by act and word unweariedly forwarded
> him as none else could in all of worthy that he
> did or attempted. She died in London, 21st
> April 1866, suddenly snatched from him, and
> the light of his life as if gone out.

Return after this to the High Street and visit the
fine old house of Dr Welsh, where Carlyle, succeed-
ing Edward Irving as tutor (and lover), taught Jane

Welsh in a little room. In the stately drawing-room, with the Adams mantelpiece and wood-panelling round the tall window which looks across the gardens to the dim blue hills, they first met. Down in that sweet old garden, they dreamed their dreams of love—or, was it only ambition? To this home of her childhood Jane Welsh returned after many years, to remember many heart-breaks. Yonder, on the garden path Carlyle stood on the day of the funeral, gazing up at the room where they first met, as if his heart would break. We never love the old man more than just then, for the frozen love had melted when the little Mocking Bird was dead. If only he had kissed her oftener during these forty years when she served him, there would have been no need to kiss a cold tombstone in the ruined aisle when it was—too late!

After this, if you wish to match the prodigious learning of Carlyle, you have only to step across to another street and go up a queer little entry, and there you will see the old manse and kirk of John Brown of Haddington—that miracle of Scots scholarship who taught himself Greek by a system of his own devising while he herded sheep near Abernethy. Like Abraham Lincoln, who had less than twelve months' schooling, John Brown had a very meagre curriculum—only a quarter or two at school and one month at Latin. Yet the church of that day suspected young Brown of troking with the devil, because he had contrived to learn Greek without a master. Alexander Moncrieff, the minister—saintly Culfargie —with all the elders, kept him under suspension for a time before they would grant him a " testificate " of membership, because he was suspected of dealing in " Black Magic."

When he was only sixteen, John Brown penned his sheep one evening, walked twenty-four miles to St Andrews, where he arrived the following morning, and entering a bookshop asked for a Greek Testament. A professor who happened to be in the shop —was it Pringle of the Greek Chair, we wonder?— looked at the rough-clad boy and noticed that he had bare feet.

" My boy, if you can read that Greek Testament you'll have it for nothing."

The herd lad read the passage correctly, got his Testament for nothing, and by supper time was reading it among his sheep. That little Greek Testament to-day is priceless, for it symbolises the Scots scholarship which has always been the glory of our frugal democracy.

Look up at that little window above the door of the manse, and who can remember without a stound of pride that John Brown studied there without a fire, and could read not only Latin and Greek, but Hebrew, Arabic, Syriac, Persian, Ethiopic, French, Spanish, Dutch, German, and Italian! Go behind and look at that quaint little kirk, and remember again that David Hume, the atheistical philosopher, once said of him—" That's the man for me—he means what he says—he speaks as if Christ was at his elbow! "

XIV

EAST LOTHIAN

THE GARDEN OF SCOTLAND

II

WITH thoughts of this prodigious scholar, who was the ancestor of many famous Browns, we take our way out of Haddington by Bothwell's Tower, and are soon spinning along the five miles of that perfectly flat road to East Linton. This road runs above the valley of the Tyne all the way. The ruined Castle of Hailes on the riverside reminds us of Bothwell, that notorious laird of Lothian, who was the blood-guilty third husband of Mary Queen of Scots. Beyond Hailes tower rises the lumpy mass of Traprain Law.

The following story has to do with a tragedy which took place on Traprain Law in very ancient times—a tragedy from which, according to the legend, great blessing flowed to Scotland in the birth of St Kentigern or Mungo the Lovable Man.

At the beginning of the sixth century, there was a pagan king called Loth who ruled over what we now call East Lothian or the Land of Loth. He had a daughter called Thenew who became a Christian and had a Christian lover of humble origin. When the secret of their love could no longer be hidden, the

outraged father according to the law of that time
ordered that his daughter should be thrown over the
steep face of Dumpender which is another name for
Traprain Law. But when this was done, the
Princess Thenew by a miracle remained unhurt and
a crystal spring sprang from the spot on which she
fell. Then the chagrined king set her adrift in a
coracle on the Firth of Forth. The frail boat drifted
out to the May Island on the ebb tide, and then
drifted back on the flood far up the Forth, until it
was washed ashore at Culross in Fife. Here, the
hapless Princess saw a fire on the shore, and creeping
towards it, gave birth to her child. She was found
by the monks of St Serf who had his dwelling there,
and the saint adopted the child as his own. He
called the boy Kentigern, which means Chief Lord,
and the lad became so dear to him that Serf called
him by the familiar name of Mungo, which means
the Lovable Man.

In due time Mungo became a monk, and wandered
far and near. On one occasion he was driven south
to Wales, and there he founded a church on the spot
where now stands St Asaph's Cathedral. Returning
to Scotland he set up his cell at Hoddam in Dumfries.
Finally he transferred his see to the banks of the
Molindinar burn, a little stream which flows into
the Clyde. On the site of his first church here stands
the great Cathedral of Glasgow to-day. His sainted
mother Thenew, like Monica the mother of St
Augustine, was his chief earthly joy, and her name
to-day is modified into the well-known name of St
Enoch.

Kentigern, or Mungo as he was more commonly

called, was known throughout the whole of Strathclyde for his saintliness, and far beyond that. He performed many miracles, according to Jocelyn the monk of Furness, who, however, lived centuries after St Mungo's death. But, some of these stories are embodied in the city arms of Glasgow to this day.

He once restored the life of a robin which had its head cut off. On a winter's night he relit the monastery fire by blowing on the frozen branch of a tree. When Queen Langueth most carelessly entrusted her wedding ring to a soldier, the king recognised it on the man's hand when he was asleep, and slipping it off cast it into the Clyde. When the Queen came to St Mungo for help in the matter, he told her to cast a fishing line into the river, and the first salmon she caught had the ring in its mouth.

These miraculous incidents were all commemorated on the seals of the Bishops of Glasgow in the twelfth and thirteenth centuries, and now they are part of the City Arms to-day.

The robin sits on the top of the tree which was frozen, and yet blazed. The salmon with the ring in its mouth appears below the tree on its back, and other two salmon act as supporters of the shield. The original motto of the city was—" Let Glasgow flourish by the preaching of the Word." But, now the motto is confined to the first three words.

On one occasion, Columba with a company of the faithful from Iona visited Kentigern or Mungo at Glasgow, and the account of that meeting is one of the poems of Scottish Church History. Dividing his monks into three bands, Columba went forward to meet the Lovable Man. When St Mungo heard of his approach, he also divided his monks into three bands, and went forward with his whole company chanting a psalm of praise. The Columban band took up the antiphonal words and sang a " Hallelujah!" When at last the two saints met, they embraced each other and exchanged pastoral staves. Then, having passed some days together in holy friendship, they parted on the green banks of the Molindinar burn, where to-day a great God's Acre surrounds the Cathedral walls.

The Lovable Man's death was a parable of his life. He passed away while purifying his body with the waters of the rivulet he loved. So also did he appear before his Lord with a clean soul.

Thus did the tragedy of Traprain bring blessing to all Scotland because St Mungo or Kentigern was the Princess Thenew's child.

The Treasure of Traprain is a story which is only a few years old. For this little hill in East Lothian was the scene of an exciting antiquarian find in 1919.

Indications were discovered on the grassy top of Traprain of very early occupation, and the Loth and Thenew legend helped to suggest that it might be worth while to explore the summit. The Society of Antiquaries of Scotland began the excavation in 1914 by permission of the Earl of Balfour who was the proprieor of the ground. That exploration was carried on during the summers of 1914 and 1915. Several floor levels and oblong hearths were found three or four feet below the surface, with certain relics of stone, bronze and iron, also shreds of pottery, which indicated occupations of the site as early as the later stone age. Coins of the Roman Emperor

Arcadius (395-408) pointed to an occupation as late as the fifth century. But, there was no trace of Roman remains.

The Great War called away all available men in 1915, and nothing further was done till April 1919, when excavations were resumed.

After a fortnight's work, the foreman was loosening the second floor foundation when he came on something which was strange to him. He brought up on the point of his tool a silver bowl, and on carefully examining the ground the workers came on a rough pit some two feet in diameter and some eighteen inches in depth. In this pit were found heaps of silver dishes, some of which were decayed through the action of sulphur in the soil, some as brittle as an egg shell, and all embedded in a purple paste which gave off an unpleasant odour.

There was no sign of any sack or box, the whole treasure having been emptied into the earthen pit without any care or preparation. The general condition of the silver was deplorable, and the barbarians who hid it must have been in great haste. Some of the silver was folded and hammered flat. Bowls were crushed, flagons trampled upon, chalices were broken and their beautiful carvings injured. The total find amounted to 160 pieces of silver and the weight was over 770 ounces, Troy weight.

Four silver coins were most fortunately discovered, one of Valens (A.D. 304-378), another of Valentinian II (A.D. 375-392), and two of Honorius (A.D. 395-423). The date of the deposit, therefore, was probably about the beginning of the fifth century or shortly after that.

When an exhaustive and scientific inventory had been made of the whole, it became evident that this unique collection of silver was the wealth of some robber band. From the presence of Teutonic relics, and the non-Saxon nature of some of them, it was thought that the booty had been brought from Gaul.

Who exactly the spoilers were we shall never know. The probability is—that they were Saxon pirates; that this beautiful silver was some of their booty from Gaul; the ransom for some captives; the loot of some wreck; or the riches from some monastery. But, all is mere conjecture.

We can only be certain of this—that the treasure was concealed hurriedly on the top of the hill; that the robbers for some reason or other had to rise and run; and that none were ever spared to return to claim it.

To-day this silver hoard is called the Treasure of Traprain, and it can now be seen in the Museum at Edinburgh—a thing of beauty and a joy for ever.

East Linton, or Preston Kirk, is the haunt of artists. In this village were born John Pettie, Martin Hardie, Arthur Melville, and others. It has all the qualities that go to the making of a painter's paradise —an ancient bridge over the Tyne, a quaint mill, and a group of mellow red-tiled houses clustering about a picturesque bend of the river, with a flat landscape whose perpetual charm consists of great level swathes of colour that blend in the misty distance under a limitless sky. A step or two down the river will bring you to the Kirk of Preston, and if you wish to find an old-world house with a fairy name, just at the back door of Linton on the Dunbar road, you will find it in Phantassie. There is a fine old mill on the farm of Phantassie, and as we stand looking at its queer red-tiled, conical roof our thoughts fly to London town, for here was born John Rennie, the great engineer who built the London Bridge in 1831. When we remember that about 30,000 vehicles and over 100,000 people pass over that bridge every day, our eyes turn to Linton Bridge and we wonder how often must John Rennie have thought of sleepy Phantassie when the roar of London was about him!

But these old tales taigle us, and we have still five miles to go before we can stand in the High Street of Dunbar.

Dunbar is often drenched in spindrift, and the ruined castle on the cliff is drenched in history. A snell place in winter is this old East Lothian town, where the nor'-east gales blow through the streets, and there is a tang of strength in the atmosphere even on this sunniest day. The sixteenth-century town house, once a prison, has now been restored, and its clean picked walls shelter an ancient cross, which stands in one corner by the entrance. Rocky shores, sandy coves, great seas tumbling in from the most restless ocean round Britain, a fine golf course, and health at every door—little wonder that Dunbar is never without visitors.

But, to a man whose soul is alive with a sense of the past, stories of olden days sough round that old castle like the ghostly winds of twilight.

Here in 1072 landed Gospatric, Earl of North-umbria, in his flight from William the Conqueror, and founded the family of the Earls of Dunbar and

March. Out yonder, by the Doon Hill of Spott, was fought the first Battle of Dunbar, when in 1296 Edward I. subdued the town and castle. On almost the same ground the second Battle of Dunbar was fought in 1650, when Cromwell defeated the Scots. Here we touch a sore point in our national history. For Leslie, the Scots general, urged on against his better judgment by a committee of clerics, deliberately descended from his safe position on the hill to a fatal one on the level ground. Scripture texts ousted Scots broad swords at Dunbar. The result was disaster. Leslie's movement gave the hard-pressed Cromwell an ecstatic joy. The battle was turned into a disgraceful rout which meant a loss of 3000 dead for the Scots and 10,000 prisoners for the English. The English lost only thirty men. We wince to-day when we remember Dunbar Drove.

If that old castle could speak it could tell us of many a grim game of Scots and English. Here Mary and Darnley supped after the murder of David Rizzio. Here, too, Mary supped with Bothwell after the murder of Darnley. Here she mounted her horse and rode to the fatal field of Carberry Hill. Three husbands, two murders, and a lost crown by the time she was twenty-six, with execution for herself at the hinder-end! Was there ever such a queen of love, mistress of beauty and daughter of danger as Mary Queen of Scots!

Round these very roads in 1745 lay a shameful litter of arms and accoutrements, as Sir John Cope and his soldiers galloped helter skelter from Prince Charlie and his Highlanders at Prestonpans. A siccar

WHITEKIRK, BEFORE THE FIRE

place of Scots frolics and bloody memories is this same Dunbar.

So we leave it by way of Belhaven and at the cross-roads turn northwards across the Tyne by Tynninghame and Binning Wood, until we reach that quiet place of ancient pilgrimage—St Mary's, Whitekirk. No wonder this place was once called Fair Knowe—for, from the little hill on which the venerable building stands there is a wide and wonderful view of the neighbouring country. Whitekirk is steeped in legendry. St Baldred built his cell here in the seventh century. Five hundred years ago, Walter Bowmaker told how an invading English soldier tried to snatch a ring from the image of the Virgin, but a crucifix fell from above and broke the wrist of the unholy thief. The ship also which bore away the precious plate and gems from Whitekirk foundered at the mouth of the Tyne. For centuries the holy well of Whitekirk was a place of pilgrimage, no fewer than 15,653 pilgrims visiting it from all nations in 1413. And here is a Vatican tale! Pope Pius himself—then a young man known to scholars as Aeneas Sylvius—came here as a pilgrim in 1435, walking all the way from Dunbar to Whitekirk on the frosty ground with his bare feet. Little wonder that he suffered ever afterwards from rheumatism.

Stand to-day in the sun, and look at the warm tints on the old red sandstone, at the pointed roof, the square tower and the crumbling porch and you will realise something of the pricelessness of this pre-reformation shrine of Mary. Then, perhaps, you will shudder at the vandalism of those fanatic women who set fire to Whitekirk in the year 1914.

K

But, time is a healer of many wounds, and Whitekirk
has been restored again.   The old monkish Tithe
Barn, which stands on the hill behind, incorporates
an ancient peel tower, which may have been part
of the original Pilgrim's House.   Truly, history
broods over Sleepy Whitekirk like the summer
silence.

To the north of Whitekirk stands the farm of
Gleghornie, the birthplace of John Major, that
Scottish scholar of European fame who taught John
Knox, Patrick Hamilton, and Gorge Buchanan.   Did
ever a man have three such pupils!   He was an
out and out mediævalist, having no troke with the
Reformed Faith.   He won for himself an almost
supernatural reputation in Paris, where Louis Coronel
of Segovia wrote: " Our Master John Major, whose
learning will commend him not only to posterity but
to Eternity."   But Robert Senalis excelled Louis,
when he added: " John Major flies on his own
wings higher than the clouds would carry him till
he passes above all spirits in Sublimity."   This son
of a humble serf at Gleghornie was the friend and
equal of Gavin Douglas, who was born in the
adjoining castle of Tantallon—in feudal times, a
wonderful proof of John Major's greatness.

When we top the hill at Auldhame what a wonderful view there is on a blue-white sunny day!
Tantallon and the Bass!   Visions rise before us at
the very names.   Tantallon—that stronghold of the
Douglases for two centuries, which later became a
state prison for such grandees as the Duchess of
Albany and the Lord of the Isles.   The Bass—that
bluff rock rising out of the sea with its ugly cliffs and

sloping roof of turf, its winking lighthouse and its bitter memories. No sea-washed island prison round our shores can compare with the Bass, whose very name spelled death. Here many a Covenanter was confined—John Blackadder, Gordon of Earlston, Alexander Peden, Fraser of Brea, and not a few lairds and ministers of the outed kirk.

" It's an unco place the Bass," said Black Andy, and no wonder.

Down at Canty Bay, the port of the Bass, that old inn has sheltered kings' men and Covenanters, smugglers from the fastnesses of the Lammermoors and pirates from the Low Countries. These golden sands, these quiet grassy braes which are covered with primroses in spring and wild flowers in summer, these silent creeks where the little waves gluck mysteriously on the dark nights—they have seen many a dastardly deed and many a good man in the throes of trouble. Tantallon, the Bass, and Canty Bay—gaze at them long enough as you sit in silence above the cove, you will feel the very creeps of history in your soul.

Three miles more and you are walking through the clean streets of that pleasant place, North Berwick. The Law dominates the little town as the Bass dominates the sea. In mediæval times North Berwick was ruled by the feudal Lords of Tantallon. A hundred years ago it was an obscure royal burgh. To-day, kings, princes, prime ministers, and all and sundry meet on the golfing greens as brothers in a democratic sport. It was that same John Major, who in 1521 wrote of women that " they ought to be kept apart from men, as it were, by a red-hot line." But now! The nunnery of the place is in ruins and fair women swing the club in daily comradeship with their lovers.

If Dunbar is a place of snell winds and angry rocks, North Berwick, with its kindlier air and miles of green links edged with sand, deals more gently with the seeker after health. The golf ball rules the town. Indeed, on the sea fringe of Haddington you cannot get away from golf, for from North Berwick, round the coast by Gullane to Aberlady, there is an unbroken series of famous links stretching for six or seven miles.

Dirleton is only a couple of miles farther on. You come suddenly on it and find it full of an old-world atmosphere. You can dream of Crusaders in Dirleton. In the twelfth-century castle of the family of De Vaux, with its fine gateway, its moat, its tortuous passages and its oubliette you have the ideal of an ancient feudal lordship, which takes you back at one leap of the imagination to the times of knight-errantry. To make the ruin all the more picturesque, it is set in gardens which blaze with colour against the sombre yew trees. At its very gates you have the church, the castle inn, peaceful cottages and a little school all grouped round a village green. Great trees throw their ageless arms about the sequestered world of Dirleton, which is surely the loveliest village in all the Lothians.

From this fairy burgh of lost romance we soon emerge on the open sweep of flat green lands round about Gullane, with glorious views across the county to the dim blue Lammermoors. Golf and Gullane come naturally to the tongue. But it was not always so. Time was when these great green links made an ideal training ground for race-horses under the famous George Dawson. The next village is Aberlady, and it is curious to remember that in olden times Aberlady was the port of Haddington; its harbour, however, was silted up long ago.

Here, the countryside is dotted with old historic houses—Luffness, which stands on the site of a fort that our friends of the Auld Alliance, the French, built in 1549 to prevent the landing of provisions for the English garrison in Haddington; Redhouse Castle or Reidspittal, the old home of the Jacobite Hamiltons; the new house of Gosford, which you can see on a clear day from the Mound in Edinburgh, and Ballencrieff, the seventeenth-century home of the Elibank Murrays.

The easiest way to return to Edinburgh is by the shore road. But the true tramp takes the longest way round. So we turn southwards to the little Garleton Hills by the road that runs past Ballencrieff. This road, to the west of the Hopetoun monument, reaches a height of four hundred and fifty feet.

At the eastern end of these hills lies a remote little village called Athelstaneford, which ought to be a place of pilgrimage to every loyal Scot. Here the Scots flag, which is the oldest of the three flags in the Union Jack, had its origin away back in the tenth century. The legend of the Chronicle has it that the Saxon King Athelstane (925-940) fought a battle on this spot against Hungus, King of the Picts, who was assisted by Achaius, King of the Scots. Before the battle our forebears prayed to God for victory. Suddenly, in answer to their prayer, a white cross in the form of the letter X appeared on the blue sky, and the Saxon King was defeated. Ever after that the Scots carried a blue flag with a white St Andrew's cross on it. This has been the flag of Scotland for nearly a thousand years. We uncover our heads at Athelstaneford and thank God for the idealism of Scotland, and for the oldest flag in the British Empire.

We give a cry to Haddington once more in the passing and take a new road home by Pencaitland and Winton Castle. Every village and mansion calls up the name of some great man of history, and only a very eident Scot would set himself to tell the story of this wonderful country which is the Garden of Scotland. There is Ormiston village, the birthplace of that famous missionary Robert Moffat, the father-in-law of David Livingstone. Yonder is Elphinstone Tower standing against the sunset sky. We began with Wishart facing Cardinal Beaton in that old keep, and we end with a vision of John Knox sitting under the yew tree at Ormiston Hall listening to George Wishart preaching. As we cross the Tyne for the last time, we say good-bye to East Lothian, feeling that the half has not been told about the delectable land which to-day is a farmer's paradise and yesterday was the battle-ground of kings.

An Englishman will pass Dunbar or Bannockburn with a calm indifference to the victories and defeats of his ancestors. But, to us there is always a sound of keening in history. The sight of Flodden, or the field of Pinkie, or the Doon Hill of Dunbar still means a wave of emotion and some bitter regrets. Lost chances and slain hopes have always wrung the finest ballads from our hearts and called an army of youth from our hearths.

They went forth to battle but they always fell.

It has been so from the first of time in this grey northern land. It will be so to the long last. Were not the bloody fields of France strewn with myriad tartans but yesterday? For, in spite of our dour silences and rough-cast ways we are idealists to the end. The Blue banner with the White Cross, although now a thousand years old, gives us joy in battle still, and *The Flowers o' the Forest* is our ageless coronach of death.

XV

ST TRIDUANA

AMONG the many places celebrated as a pilgrim
shrine, in and around Edinburgh, none is more
interesting than the Holy Well of St Triduana, at
Restalrig. Comparatively few citizens have even
heard her name, and yet this godly woman set an
ideal for womanhood which every daughter of the
twentieth century would do well to worship.

The name Triduana appears in many forms—
Treddles, Tredwell, Trallew, Trallen, Tradlius, and
Tradwell. But it is quite useless to look for con-
sistency in the various versions of a medieval story.

One version tells us that the glorious virgin
Triduana of Colossae, along with other two virgins,
Potentia and Emeria, came over the sea to Scotland
in the company of St Regulus or St Rule, the famous
monk of Constantinople, who bore with him the
bones of St Andrew, and landed at Kilrymont, which
is the old name for St Andrews. Triduana settled
at Rescobie, in Angus, where she became a recluse.
Another version tells us that she and Crescentia
came to Pictland with St Bonifacius and settled at
Restenneth, which is in Rescobie parish, two miles
north-east of Forfar. The ruins of Restenneth

Priory still stand, and in Rescobie there used to be
a fair called St Triduana's Fair. As far north as the
Island of Papa Westray in the Orkneys there is the
ruin of another chapel called St Tredwell's Church,
and October 8 in the Roman calendar is sacred to
St Tredwell or St Triduana.

Any contradictory statements in the various
versions of this old legend matter little to us
compared with the one outstanding tradition that
Nectan, King of the Picts, conceived a violent passion
for Triduana, which made it necessary for her to
flee from Angus. She journeyed west, and settled
in secret at Dunfallandy, near Pitlochry, in Perth-
shire. But the ambassadors of the King found her
out and entreated her to return.

" What does so great a prince desire of me, a poor
virgin dedicated to God? " said Triduana.

" He desireth the most excellent beauty of thine
eyes, which if he obtain not he will assuredly die,"
they replied.

" Then what he seeketh that shall he assuredly
have," answered Triduana.

And, plucking out her eyes, she skewered them on
a thorn and handed them to the King's Ministers,
who were horrified.

" Take that which your Prince desireth," said the
saintly virgin.

The King, on receiving the thorn-pierced eyes,
greatly admired the perfection of her sacrifice, and
from that day she was no more troubled with
amorous pursuit. She was now free to devote herself
to prayer, and settled down in a cell at Restalrig,
in Lothian. There she lived until she died, and was

buried where Restalrig Church now stands.   So St
Triduana is not only a Scots saint, but she is peculiarly
an Edinburgh saint.

As we can well imagine, St Triduana was soon
invoked by all who were blind, or who had some
grievous affection of the eyes.   Sir David Lindsay
tells us of people going to St Tredwell " to mend
their ene."   He also speaks of Triduana's image at
Restalrig, with the thorn transfixing the two eyeballs.
But at the Reformation is was ordained " that the
Kirk at Restalrig, as a monument of idolatrie, be
raysit and utterlie cast down and destroyed."

St Triduana's tomb, and her Holy Well adjacent,
became the most celebrated place of pilgrimage in
the Lothians.   Many miracles were said to be
wrought there by the influence of the saint, both in
her life-time and after her death.   It must have been
a pathetic place of pilgrimage, for the blind were led
to Restalrig and all who had any ophthalmic trouble.
When the saint died a little church must have been
raised over her tomb.

But, leaving legendary, we now come to the
concrete facts of history.

The Norman family of the De Restalrigs built a
Norman church here, on the site of the primitive
shrine, before the days of Alexander III.   Restalrig
Church was erected into a collegiate establishment
and rebuilt by James III., as it is stated in a Papal
Bull of the year 1487.   James IV. added greatly to
its riches, and endowed an extra chaplain in 1512.
Twelve years later, James V. added still another
rectory to its already great riches.   About the same
time a chapel was built, or rebuilt, to enclose the

Well of Triduana, with beautiful Gothic stonework, which still exists.

This well of St Triduana and the Well of St Margaret, which stood within a few hundred yards of it in Clockmill Lane, were the two most beautiful covered wells in Scotland. But the stonework of the Well of St Margaret was removed to the King's Park to make room for the engine-works erected by the North British Railway, which are now called St Margaret's Works.

When first I saw the Well of Triduana, the crypt-like building at the side of the church was covered by a conical turf roof. But the Well was cleaned out in 1908, and the building above it, with its vaulted roof, restored by the Earl of Moray. The outer roof is now a seemly slated cone, on the apex of which there stands a little effigy in stone of St Triduana—

"Quhilk on ane thorn has baith her ene."

But, how few Edinburgh folk or tourists, looking out of the train window as they pass by Restalrig, ever notice that tiny image of the Saint, or are acquainted with the tragic story of her thorn-pierced eyes?

It is interesting to note that, as late of the year 1920, certain pious Roman Catholics with ophthalmic trouble, travelled from Glasgow during the Trades Holiday to Restalrig on a pilgrimage, and asked the church officer about the Holy Well of St Triduana. Alas! The waters of the well have long been diverted by the draining of the adjacent meadows.

The Well of Margaret, Scotland's Queen and

Saint, stood in the Clockmill Lane where the railway
engine works stand to-day. A fine old elder tree
spread its covering over the grass-grown roof of the
well, and a thatched cottage stood in front of it.
When the railway works were built, some time in the
'seventies of last century, the fine building which
covered the well was removed, stone by stone, and
re-erected over the ancient spring which flows at the
foot of Salisbury Crags opposite Holyrood, and not
far from St Anthony's Chapel. This is now called
St Margaret's Well.

It will repay anyone to examine this medieval
building to-day. The hexagonal roof rises to a height
of five feet, and a stone ledge or seat runs round five
of the sides, a little above the water. The sixth side
makes the arched entrance to the well. From the
centre of the crystal clear water a round pillar rises
and splays out into a groined roof—the ribs of the
roof rising from corbels which are set out at angles of
the building. The water must have flowed in olden
times from the mouth of a grotesque figure at the
head of the central shaft, but now it flows from a
leaden pipe which is fixed into the gargoyle's mouth.
On a bright summer day the sparkling water
illumines the dark roof, giving the whole interior a
sense of radiant coolness.

Let us be very thankful that when the railway
works were built over the holy well in Clockmill
Lane, this fine example of a medieval well-covering
was removed to Arthur Seat, and not destroyed.

XVI

THE RETREAT

A HAUNT OF PEACE ON THE WHITADDER

BLESSED is the man who knows of some quiet retreat where he can hide himself when the racket of affairs threatens to overset his sanity. Who does not know the feeling of being burdened by some mysterious weight on awaking from sleep? Then, it dawns on us that it is only the thought of the day's work that has filled us with an apprehension that should not be there. When that happens, we have lost the joy of living, and it is time for us to be off.

.   .   .   .

It was a blue May day morning. Within an hour or two of awaking, the car drew in to the side of a grassy field above a river that threads its way through the heart of the Lammermoors. The old Round House stood before us, with its white, three feet thick walls. All the chimneys emerge from the centre of the conical roof. A quaint covered passage runs from the house to the kitchens and the diningroom on one side, and on the other a group of outhouses snuggle alongside the rounded wall. Its stance on the riverside is perfect—flat meadow lands of old turf dotted with ancient trees. The long, pointed, ecclesiastical-like windows wink in the morning sun at a high bank across the river, and not far beyond are the heathery slopes of Cockburn Law. Behind the house there is a trim garden with clipt shrubs and a tiny avenue, and further down the riverside a big old-fashioned garden is enclosed within a high circular wall. When we sauntered through this paradise of peace, the river was making one long hush of music, and in the quiet pools the trout were playing.

Here, surely, on this hot morning we had come on the dream-house of a hermit, far sequestered from the world, and well named The Retreat, where it was easy to forget that there were men driving hard bargains and puckering their brows over money columns in the distant city.

The friend who brought us here was born in the old Round House, and his happiness was complete when the rods were unpacked and he had pulled on his waders. The last touch was added to forgetfulness when he began to throw a perfect line, and the long cast glistened in the sun with a rhythmic beauty. From that moment, all through the live-long day, until the evening called us home, the worries of work and the markets of the world did not exist for any of us.

When the fisherman was a boy, family prayers were said in the White House at nine o'clock sharp every evening. But, once after a fruitless fishing, the " rise " began in the home pool just as nine was chapping on the old clock. The boy had to toss up between the trout and the Book, and—the trout won. So he fished on and on, until he landed his thirteenth in the dark within a stone's throw of the judgment bar! Then he went home, happy and resigned, to face the music. Alas! his father was not a fisherman, and did not understand. But, it was worth it all.

In those days the boy used only one fly on his line—the Partridge. To-day the man used five flies on his cast—Black Spider, Greenwell's Glory, Woodcock, and Hairlug, with Dun Spider for a tail fly. But he has been faithful to his friend of long ago, for the Partridge still comes first. Certainly he is a good fisherman, for 41 trout lay on the primrose bank at the end of the day.

We walked down stream by the upper and laigh haughs. The river here is all that a stream should be—long runs of broken water, a swirling tail to the big pools, still amber-brown stretches without a ripple, little falls, and a roaring gorge, where the water struggles for freedom between the rocks opposite Elba.

Here the tiny Otterburn falls into the river, and the path leads up through the woods by the old copper mines to a sawmill and the white gate on the road. Or you can cross the swing bridge, and from the further bank get a glimpse of Cockburn Law, and the young larch trees greening in beauty.

There was May music on every side. Blackbirds fluting luscious songs, willow warblers making little cataracts of melodious laughter, the hollow challenge of cock pheasants, the great tit working his musical saw, the wandering voice of the cuckoo, the bleat of lambs, and behind all, the constant hush of the river as it flashed past in the sun.

And what colour of May was there! A blue-white sky above. The warm red earth of the riverside haughs, delicately brairded with every shade of

verdure. A green mist in the woods, making a fairy
atmosphere which was not yet dense enough to hide
the tracery of the branches—for the trees in the first
flush of spring stand up like men who have not yet
lost all their character by over-bourgeoning. Swathes
of white anemonies and banks of yellow primroses
make the secret glades of these woods more
gorgeously carpeted than a king's palace, for no
outrageous hand destroys them in this sanctuary of
nature. A white cloud of blackthorn blossom lies on
the banks across the stream, and sweet violets peep
between the primrose tufts. The water laughs and
sparkles in the sun; the blue sky is reflected in every
wavelet, or turns the still pools into planes of
sapphire. On the spit of shingle at the bend below
the old house, a thin blue column of reek rises from
the fire where we eat our lunch in the midday heat,
and the warm air is filled with the pungent scent of
burning pinewood. Later in the season the kingfisher
darts, like a blue flame, across yon bosky bank above
the deep water.

Surely God made all this colour and music and
beauty of Spring that men might forget for a little
while their tempers and their toils and renew their
souls in the sheer joy of living!

When the afternoon sun was at its hottest I
retraced my steps along the mossy turf in front of
the Round House. A French window stood open
between two tall auricarias, and in the still afternoon,
when the cushies were dovering in the great trees,
the sound of men's voices floated through the
window like an echo from the unseen world—a
London choir, doubtless, whose singing was wafted to

this quiet place on winds invisible by that miracle of our age—wireless. Mammoth pine trees, with arms that branched upwards like the sevenfold candlesticks of Jewry, stood on the green flats by the side of the river. The path then continues upstream through the woods, and there is no stretch of Tweed itself more beautiful than this reach of the Whitadder from Coppermines to Abbey St Bathans.

What a primrose path it is through the spring woods! It rises high above the river, and you can watch the wild ducks sporting in the clear water below. Here, too, is the haunt of many squirrels. The primroses are prodigal. Indeed, at one place the yellow edge of the river bank meets the blue line of the running water in one long kiss of colour. Here might one spend the livelong day in picking anemonies, primroses, wood sorrel, violets, and lady's mantle fresh bursting into flower.

At the end of the wood you cross an old road that leads down to a ford, and then take an open path along the braeface among the golden gorse. Descending to the riverside again, you hear the long heart-some hum of a sawmill across the water. The drowsy sound would send you to sleep if only you lay down on the warm bank. A white butterfly flits across the path, and up the little stream on the right stands the country school. What lessons might not a child learn in such a college of nature!

Just then I saw a girl and boy standing with two spotless white meal pokes by the wire and pulley trolley which crosses the river here to the trim houses on the other side. They pulled the wooden box across on the wire, opened it, took out a number of

L

white loaves, filled their sacks, and then sent the box
back again on the wire to the other side. What an
idyllic way of bringing home the bread! The laird's
house is half-hidden by the trees on the further side
of the water, an aggregate of chimneys and pepper-
box turrets, with windows looking upstream to the
old kirk.

The grassy path continues alongside a little coppice
that separates you from the river. There was not a
breath of wind to temper the heat; the gean trees
were shedding their blossoms like showers of summer
snow; and the warm air was heavy with the scent of
flowers and trees and all the nameless outbreathings
of the spring. When I crossed the swing bridge
which leads to the village and the old kirk, the
evening light was sklenting, and the close of day was
made holy with the litany of blackbirds and thrushes.
The whole rivervale was full of peace and beauty.

I crossed the bridge and sat down in the kirkyard
among the graves. The trout were plopping in the
still water, the bleat of a lamb came down from the
hill, and in a garden close by there was the constant
click of a spade. In the sunny silence I sat and
wondered that one of Columba's holy men should
have carried the torch all the way from Iona into this
obscure valley of the Lammermoors. Yet here am
I to-day, sitting among the graves of an old parish
kirk which is the true successor of the little cell that
was founded in the name of Baithene, son of Brendan,
first cousin and immediate follower of Columba
himself in the sacred Isle of Hy. How much is
preserved in a name? For Baithene died over
thirteen hundred years ago, and still we call this

" ecclesia sancti Baythani "—Abbey St Bathans to-day.

As I wandered slowly back to The Retreat, I grudged the passing of this tranquil day. Beauty, peace, and instant pleasure had mingled with a sense of ancient things, memories of half-forgotten saints, and ballad days that will come again no more.

XVII

PENTLAND HAUNTS OF
ROBERT LOUIS STEVENSON

A Scotsman never thinks of hills but he hears a whaup. When a Scot is exiled in other lands or on those distant islands of the sea which lie beyond the margin of the world, the very thought of home will often hurt him with that sweetest of all life's pains— the pain of love, for which there is no anodyne save home.

Robert Louis Stevenson was an exiled Scot. The happiest hunting-grounds of dream to him were these neighbourly Pentland Hills, which lie at the very backdoor of Edinburgh. Lovers of Stevenson have again and again acquainted themselves with every local reference in his works to Swanston and the Pentlands. As his Hills of Home they are now proverbial throughout the world. For on those rolling tops he often stood and viewed our grey castled city by the sea, reeking blue in the morning sun—that New Jerusalem of the fighting Scot which has risen from the cloor and clash of centuries rather than descended from any mystical heaven. It is unnecessary now for anyone to catalogue the passages in Stevenson which make mention of Swanston and the Pentlands. The only thing left to us is that which is always left to a lover. We may try to

THE HILLS OF HOME

recapture the atmosphere of the old days and the old songs, to dream ourselves back and think aloud, like him, until we feel the very hurt of love which the exile felt on the lone Pacific isle when he shut his eyes and heard, as in the days of long ago, the hill birds calling above the well on Halkerside: —

> The whaup's wild cry on the breeze blawn by
> Like a wandering word frae hame.

But the very throngness of Swanston to-day is a fine memorial to Stevenson. The summer visitors who haunt the clachan and the hill; the pilgrims who peer through the gate and over the garden wall, the very policeman who stands on a Saturday or Sunday in summer time near the Roaring Shepherd's Cottage like a uniformed incarnation of John Todd himself, most uncomfortable in his silver buttons and blue coat, come back, as it were, to herd stranger sheep than the ewes and lambs that bleated and baa'd about the braes of Swanston in his day—how all this new vogue of the Pentland Hills and the happy fame of Swanston would astonish Stevenson if he slipped back from the other side! He might even be mistaken among the crowd for a gangrel body, and turned away on a wet day from his own door because he did not look respectable, if, in his shabby coat and long hair falling over his ears, he chapped for a piece—he who once wrote with a chuckle in his soul this wise word for the over-conventional gentry of Auld Reekie: " Respectability—the deadliest gag and wet blanket that can be laid on man."

An old Highlander once said to me, " You can

never win close to the spirit of the hills till you climb high, all your lone, where there is no one else to break the thrum." And it was because Stevenson wandered about these Hills of Home alone, dreaming the long, happy dreams of youth, which stirred all the romantics in his soul, or listening to John Todd's philosophy of the sheep-folds—that fell shepherd, whose wrathful voice was like an " audible bogie "—skulking, too, in his favourite wilderness like a Cameronian in the killing times—thus, and thus alone, did he enter into the meaning and mystery of the life of men and things, shepherds and sheep, great folks and simple, hills and gardens, the high gests of love and the deep dolours of grief, and the homely talk of folks about the doors.

Happy too are we to-day if, in trying to bring back Stevenson's world, we have our own heartsome memories of his Pentland haunts. To enter the magic door of the cottage as a friend, in the fine free days when a well-known Lord of Session, himself an acquaintance of Stevenson, made the place a very howf of pilgrims, with portraits of Braxfield and Cummy looking down from the walls, and a rowth of Stevenson relics everywhere. To sit in the shepherd's kitchen supping kail or eating beefsteak pie in happy days and sad, at the fireside of John Todd's successor, whose twinkling eyes and lilting, lallan tongue are good to see and hear. To walk home with the ghost of Louis in the small hours under the white light of a harvest moon, from a wedding feast in the barn, when the sound of music and dancing kept the hoolets in the farm garden in a state of open-eyed alarm, and filled the hearts of the old, rosy-faced

country folks with memories of their own courtings
in the auld lang syne. To range these hills from
end to end in lonely glamourie, with Stevenson
guiding our feet to his own favourite haunts. Only
thus can we also enter into the soul of the lad that
is gone.

Swanston Cottage needs no describing to those
Stevenson lovers who have seen it. And yet it is a
grievous thing to a stravaiging Scot that so many live
to-day in Stevenson's city who have never seen this
paradise within a wall. This quaint old eighteenth-
century junketing house of the Edinburgh bailies,
where long ago the city fathers laid primitive wooden
water pipes, and, later, built a water-house to
preserve the springs in the garden. What jovial days
and nights our municipal ancestors must have spent
there, with the finest of Pentland water to mellow
their drinks! Then those wise councillors enlarged
the cottage, and robbing the old Cathedral of St
Giles, at its vandal restoration, of some of its
gargoyles and crockets, set them up to ornament
the new-made garden. Here among the roses and
gillyflowers, there came a lad in the year 1867 to
dream and scribble and laze his time away in the
best of all literary apprenticeships—ruminating and
reading and letting his imagination rove freely, while
the seven sisters of Caerketton looked down on him,
through the long summer nights, where the old
drove roads wind over the hills and far away.

Stevenson would often moon about the grey old
farmhouse standing in its " bouquet of trees." Here
there was an added glamour in the fact that on this
spot there once stood a grange of the good monks of

Whitekirk. With that dreamy eye of his he saw in these very fields the rosy friars tilling the soil. He saw, too, the farm door standing open all night in the killing times to welcome many a hunted Covenanter. He saw, later still, in the Forty-five, Charlie's wild Highlanders surrounding Swanston in the dawn and plucking the very blankets from the bed of a little child who sat up in fear and watched the royal thieves mixing their " braw brose " with cream from the dairy. What a fine translator of history was this lanky lad with the delicate air, who filled his lungs with the heather-scented winds of Swanston, transforming the dry-as-dust details into brave pictures and moving stories, which were to delight the hearts of later generations.

Of all the Stevenson shrines in or around Edinburgh this " place in the dell " is the most romantic —Swanston, the home of his heart, the happy nursery of his literary labours, and the place of pilgrimage for many a lover of *Tusitala* from the far lands beyond the seas.

I make no doubt that he would often step eastward across the fields and sit among the graves of Old Pentland Churchyard—that place of hallowed memories for a Presbyterian Scot like Stevenson, in whose veins ran the blood of the Covenant. And yet—although it is almost within sight of Swanston, few now know, as he must have known, the holy romance of this ancient God's Acre. As I sit here on a May day afternoon among the graves, remote from the world that flies past on the distant turnpike road, the air is melodious with the song of larks soaring above the brairded fields. A steep grass-grown approach, a row of ancient yews, a handful of tombs, cowslips in the grass, your back to a red blaes bing, and your face to the green slopes of his own Kirk Yetton—the sough of the Covenant comes to you like the wind sighing in the yew trees. For here is the gravestone of little Beatrix Umpherston, who, in the year 1683, when only ten years of age, was the first of fifteen godly bairns in Pentland to sign *The Children's Bond.*

> This is a Covenant made between the Lord and us, with our whole hearts, and to give up ourselves freely to Him, without reserve, soul and body, heart and affections, to be His children, and Him to be our God and Father, if it please the Holy Lord to send His gospel to the land again.

Sweet Beatrix Umpherston! How this headstone which bears her name and the name of her goodman, Mr John M'Neil, preacher in Loanhead, would send Stevenson into a dwam of history and bring the little lass of ten to his very side.

But a favourite walk was from Fisher's Tryst, by the Old Kirk of Glencorse—to-day one of the most haunting spots near Edinburgh. He sometimes went to a service there with his father, who listened with rapt attention to every word that old Mr Torrance, the minister, said.

Glencorse Kirk was Stevenson's *petit poeme en prose,* as he calls it—that little cruciform place, with its steep slate roof, its wooden steeple, and its kirkyard, full of graves. One grey headstone to Charles Cottier, a Frenchman from Dunkerque, who died a prisoner at the military prison hard by;

another, " the most pathetic memorial I ever saw—
a poor school slate in a wooden frame, with the
inscription cut into it, evidently by the father's hand.
In church old Mr Torrance preached—over eighty,
and a relic of times forgotten, with his black thread
gloves, and mild, old, foolish face. One of the
nicest parts of it was to see John Inglis, the greatest
man in Scotland, our Justice-General, and the only
born lawyer I ever heard, listening to the piping old
body, as though it had all been a revelation, grave
and respectful."

Little did the boy from Swanston think of the
fame he was to bring to this ruined kirk.

The inscriptional gem of the place stands at the
eastmost end, and has on it this poem carved by a
humourless husband in memory of his dead spouse:

> Death is not care, it is not pain,
>   But it is rest and peace;
> Death makes all our terrors vain
>   And bids our torments cease.
>
> This stone is for to mark the ground
>   Where Mary Simpson lies,
> Lawful wife to John M'Kean,
>   Till death did close her eyes.
>
> Departed life at Marfield Lodge
>   The sixteenth of July,
> Eighteen hundred and forty-two,
>   Where she did calmly die.

To-day, the Kirk of Glencorse is roofless, with
ivy covering the walls, and green grass flooring the
little nave, with the open sky above, where not long
ago a piper played laments within the walls, on a

radiant June day, with thoughts in his mind of the great Justice-General, old Mr Torrance, the French prisoner, little Catherine Ogg, the seven-month-old bairn, whose name is cut on the school slate, and Robert Louis, the lad that is gone. The steep incline to the old kirk; the well-worn sandstone steps by the swing gate which have been scooped hollow by the feet of generations, and the little burn, downby, must have been in Stevenson's thoughts when he asked S. R. Crockett to go some sunny June Sunday, and say a prayer for him with closed eyes. " I will never walk by the Fisher's Tryst and Glencorse. I shall never see Auld Reekie. I shall never set my foot again on the heather. Here I am until I die, and here will I be buried." In that letter you have the Pentland memories which hurt Stevenson with a twist of pain—an exile's hankering after love's lost days, that only home can satisfy.

Stevenson had a Covenanting childhood, and it was all due to his nurse, Cummy. He wrote long afterwards from Samoa, " My style is from the Covenanting writers." Hackston of Rathillet, sitting on his horse, resolving his doubts, with the cloak about his mouth, watching the murder of Archbishop Sharpe on Magus Moor, fascinated him. So, before he was fifteen, he wrote a novel on the subject, tried the same thing again, wasting reams of paper, but without any approved success. He next tried a novel on the Pentland Rising, for when staying as a boy in Colinton manse, he would lie awake at night thinking of that ragged army of the Covenant which spent the night before the battle, within a stone's throw of his bed. But he failed again. Then, when he was sixteen, came a little green pamphlet on "The Pentland Rising," published anonymously in 1866 by Andrew Elliot in Edinburgh. His father thought nothing of it, and bought up all the copies. To-day the little green pamphlet is a Stevensonian treasure for the book-collector.

As we climb the steep fields on the lower slopes to the east of Turnhouse Hill, we see the Rullion Green monument standing within a railing in front of a wood. Here Stevenson's earliest imagination was fired as he wandered these history-haunted braes. He knew all the facts. He had already read the authorities. In his pamphlet he described the cause of the revolt, when M'Lelland of Barscob shot Corporal Deanes of Dalry, in Galloway, for attempting to roast alive an old man. He tells us that out of M'Lelland's pistol had been fired ten pieces of a tobacco pipe into the body of Deanes. He described the march of that first pathetic army of the Covenant from Dumfries by Lanark and Bathgate to Colinton, with Dalyell of Binns on their heels. Rain and frost and snow made miserable going over pitiful broken moors for this ill-prepared peasant corps. Some turned back, and others, fearful of being unfaithful, tied themselves together. All were more or less without hope of success. The Lothian folks gave no help. The terrible weather did the rest. Many of these men had little else than a sword or an old musket in their hands, and a meal poke on their backs. In a wretched bivouac within Colinton kirk-yard they lay all night in frost and snow. Next day they swung round the hillfoots by Dreghorn Castle, Swanston, Fulford (Woodhouselee), and

GLENCORSE OLD KIRK

Flotterstone Bridge to the old market stance of Rullion Green, on the south-east base of Turnhouse Hill, where many a ragged *rullion* had been gathered to the cattle tryst at House of Muir, a market which is mentioned in the *Scots Act of Parliament* as early as 1581. Ragged in pelt and dirty in cloot, they looked like hunted sheep that had escaped a shearing —veritable *rullions*, as Ayrshire folk style uncouth, tousy characters to this day.

Meanwhile, Dalyell of Binns made hot haste over the hills of Pentland by the drove road from Currie, between Capelaw and Bellshill, through the Maidens Cluch, past Kirkton and St. Cathrine's Chapel, which is now submerged by the waters of the Glencorse Reservoir. Yonder, between Lawhead and Turnhouse, he spied the miserable little army of 900 waiting, on their well-chosen vantage ground, to face his 3000 regular troops. There, the last stand of the Covenanters was made on this fatal 28th day of November 1666, while two preachers of the Word— Welsh and Semple—called aloud the slogans of Judah to encourage their doomed brethren, and the strains of the 71st and 78th Psalms went soughing down the winter wind. They had only sixty muskets, forty pairs of pistols, and twenty pounds of loose powder. But they made great play when it came to a hand-to-hand tulzie. Were ever men in such a desperate case? Did ever Scots fight more gallantly in a losing battle? The tale has been told a hundred times. But still our hearts heave with emotion when we think of the slaughter in the gathering dusk, of the scores lying wounded when the sun went down, of the trodden snow seeping with blood. Many of the fugitives were cruelly murdered, and one hundred and twenty were taken prisoners. When the moon rose the soldiers stripped the bodies of the slain, but next day the godly women of Edinburgh went out with fine household linen and buried the dead in shrouds in a grave over which the present monument stands. All through that bitter night there was a sound of galloping hooves, and the moors and glens of Pentland were full of the silent, hurrying figures of men who sought hiding and shelter for dear life.

Is it any wonder that Stevenson's early imaginations were stirred by this brave, forlorn tale of the Covenant? How his boyish soul must have been thrilled when first he heard from Cummy's lips or read in a book the story of that big, lion-hearted, old campaigner, Captain John Paton of Meadowhead—galloping off on his horse with three soldiers thundering after him! The soldiers ride so fast that they are soon up with him. One of them actually tries to catch his cloak. In front of them is a wide, treacherous mossy pool, out of which three Covenanters are already pulling their plunging ponies. The soldiers see it. Paton puts his great horse to the pool. A mighty leap and both horse and rider land safely on the other side. A swing round. A drawn sword flashes, and John Paton splits the head of the first cavalier as he struggles in the morass. The other two come tumbling over the horse and body of their dead companion, until the pool is hottering with dead or dying men and beasts.

" Take my compliments to your master and tell

him I cannot sup with him to-night," cries John Paton as he gallops off into the night, with a thunder of hooves on the hill.

Twelve miles over the hills to the west, as the crow flies, there stands to-day on Blacklaw Hill a Covenanter's grave, a place which must have been well-known to Stevenson. It is the grave of a fugitive from Rullion Green who was making his way, wounded and weary, to his home in Ayrshire. But at dead of night, after the battle, his strength failed. So he crept painfully to the lonely farm-house of Blackhill, and tapped on the window. Out came Adam Sanderson and begged him to come in-by. But the dying man would not endanger his kindly host, and begged only that he would convoy him up the valley of the West Water. Then, falling exhausted at the dawn, he died in Adam Sanderson's arms, with this last word whispered in his ear— " Bury me somewhere within sight of my Ayrshire hills! " The wish itself was a covenant. So Adam Sanderson carried the dead man up to the top of Blacklaw Hill, and there, when the sunrise was tipping with gold the distant Ayrshire hills, he buried the Covenanter on the braeface and raised a little cairn to mark the spot. Yonder to-day on the lonely hill this unknown soldier of the Cross sleeps well, beaking fornent the sun, in the place where he wished to be, and within sight of his own dear hills of home.

The last known place in Pentland which we associate with Stevenson's name is the Cauldstane Slap. Not because in " Weir of Hermiston " he lifted both the Covenanter's grave and the Cauld-

stane Slap, as well as old Mr Torrance, and placed
them elsewhere to suit his romantic whim, as he
lifted the Torran Rocks in " Kidnapped " and sunk
them nearer Mull—but because as early as 1869
he had written a rough unfinished ballad of a girl
meeting her outlawed lover at the Cauldstane Slap,
from which the poem was to take its name. So
this wandering son of Swanston must surely have
found the grave on Blacklaw Hill for himself and
climbed the sombre Slap between the East and West
Cairn Hills. For the Stevenson who roamed these
hills was the buoyant lad in whose soul Cummy's
nursery tales of the Covenanters rang like the owercome of an old song to the hinmost day of life.

He never pictured Edinburgh but he painted the
Pentlands in the background to show off the city's
charms. When he wrote to his friends, the Pentlands were ever his Hills of Dream. All the love
and memories of his early days were bound up with
these haunted uplands where long ago the Covenanters fought, and drovers huddled their cattle
beasts, and shepherds buchted their sheep in summer
sun or winter storm. There was homesickness in
his heart and a mist of tears in his eyes when he
wrote these words, which express better than any
other his deathless love for this old grey land of
battle-cries and Covenants: —

Blows the wind to-day and the sun and the rain are
    flying,
  Blows the wind on the moors to-day and now,
Where above the graves of the martyrs the whaups are
    crying
  My heart remembers how!

Grey recumbent tombs of the dead in desert places,
  Standing stones on the vacant wine-red moor,
Hills of sheep, and the howes of the silent vanished races,
  And winds austere and pure:

Be it granted me to behold you again in dying,
  Hills of home! and to hear the call,
Hear about the graves of the martyrs the peewees crying,
  And hear no more at all.

M

XVIII

THE ROARING SHEPHERD
AND HIS DOGS

WITH A POEM BY HIS SON

It was a peching Pentland day. The July sun blazed down on the back without mercy. The very winds were warm as they came whiffing down the stifling ravine which leads up the North Esk Burn from Carlops to Fairliehope. At the Brownie's Pool a great temptation to take a plunge was heroically resisted. But, once across the divot bridge and up on the heights the wind blew cooler. It was pleasant then to sit down and dream awhile over the superb view down the valley and across the woodlands of the plain to the dim blue Moorfoot Hills.

The hills have lured me on to many a queer employ, but never before did I take this way of the Bore Stone to Listonshiels in such a pother of heat to find a poet and to beg a poem. The day itself was a perfect pastoral—larks warbling in the sky, yellow-hammers singing happy songs in the little trees, whinchats flying fussily to and fro, lambs bleating to their mothers on the great green hills, a hush of falling water in the burn below, and whaups gurling across the heather. Then the gleam of the loch, like a sapphire stone of deepest blue in a setting

of emerald green, a house by the waterside well
bielded by some trees, the homely sounds of cocks
and hens, and the burly figure of a man with a white
beard waving a welcome with his stick from the
gable-end.

Here lives William Todd, one of the sons of
the Roaring Shepherd of Swanston, whom Robert
Louis Stevenson immortalised. How it would have
delighted the heart of Louis to find a poet of the
purest Scots in the son of his shepherd friend! It
was a blessed relief to step out of the blazing sun
into the cool dark parlour. There is no welcome in
the world like a Scots handshake and the sound of
the mother tongue.

" A lonely life up here among the hills? "

" Ay, but it mak's ye whiles think o' things."

And that is just the reason why a hillman is so
often a philosopher and a poet.

William Todd lived with his father at Swanston
until he was fifteen years of age, and then he came
to a herding down yonder at the Carlops. The first
Sunday after leaving home he went to Carlops Kirk.
When he left Swanston his father had given him a
dog called " Trusty "; but when the boy was in the
kirk " Trusty " made off for home over the hills,
and the young herd was glad to follow him. When
the young Carlops herd left Swanston at the age of
fifteen, Robert Louis Stevenson had not yet come
to live at the cottage; but William Todd was often
home after that, and was well acquaint with the lanky
lad with the long hair and the dreamy eyes.

It was on a fine Saturday of June that William
Todd stood up at the door of the Roaring Shepherd's

cottage at Swanston and recited a poem on " Swanston's Whinny Knowes " to a large gathering of the Robert Louis Stevenson Club. The poem, with its fine Scots and its unique recollections of life at Swanston sixty years ago, captivated some of our hearts on that sunny day. Sib souls need no introduction, and an appointment was soon made to pay a visit to the lonely house among the hills. Hence this sweltering walk to the North Esk Reservoir.

The collogue in the cottage was after our own hearts and I came away that day with a big paper parcel under my arm and the poem in my pocket. The brown paper concealed an old-fashioned picture in a frame. It was the portrait of John Todd, the Roaring Shepherd—a fell likeness of that granite-faced man, and a precious loan to me.

The poem on Swanston, which has never been published, gives us a realistic description of life in the hamlet under the hill, of the tiny cottage behind the school where the shepherd of Robert Louis Stevenson lived, and of the " Pailace " next to it, that old stone bigging, which had to be shored up with an ash tree—the humble home of Mysie.

Two dogs are mentioned in the poem—" Cheviot " and " Snag." In the estimation of the shepherd, " Cheviot " was the wiser of the two, but in that case he must have been the wisest dog in Christendom. For the tradition of " Snag's " uncanny gifts is still alive. He went every week to the Edinburgh Market with John Todd, and could pen the sheep in record time. Once, when another shepherd with a silly dog was finding it ill work to pen his sheep, he asked the Roaring Shepherd to lend him " Snag."

The dog went to work, and had all the sheep in the pen immediately.

" Man," said the strange shepherd, " that's an unco dowg! "

" Ay," roared John Todd, " he could drive sheep up the bore o' a gun."

Even when John Todd did not go to the market, " Snag " would slip away by himself on the right day with the lust of labour in him, work the sheep of other shepherds at the usual pens, and come home again. " Snag " had the gift of mathematics, for he knew the seven days of the week, and he never mistook the market day.

In later life " Snag " was given to a shepherd at Biggar. It is a long day's tramp from Biggar to Edinburgh for a gangrel body, let alone a dog. But when the market day came round, " Snag," who must have calculated the time required for the journey, rose at some unearthly hour, or started the day before from the Biggar hirsel, travelled the thirty miles all alone, appeared at the Edinburgh market at the usual time, worked sheep all day at the pens, looked for his old master in vain, and then limped back to Swanston that night. The effort was too much for the old dog, and he never did any good after that. For brains, faithfulness, love of work, and sheer affection, how much better is a good sheep dog than the average man! It would lighten life for some of us if we thought that somewhere in the Elysian fields we would see our old dogs again, and pat them on the head. O John Todd, why did you ever part with " Snag " to the Biggar herd, even for a day or two?

In the photograph John Todd is sitting with the third dog—" Trusty "—between his knees. A beautiful collie, he sits as steady as a stone, with his head turned to one side. It was this same " Trusty " that ran home to Swanston, by way of Turnhouse, Glencorse, and Allermuir, when the home-sick lad William Todd was sitting in Carlops Kirk with a lump in his throat. Like lad, like dog, they were both glad to meet, that same Sunday night in the Roaring Shepherd's cottage behind the school at Swanston.

In the photograph, John Todd, the shepherd of Stevenson's memories, is seen sitting on a stone by the wall of a house near his own cottage. He has on his head a round cap with a black glazed skip to shade the eyes, a plaid of shepherd tartan about his shoulders, sheep shears in one hand, the birn or iron stamp for marking sheep in the other hand, with the farmer's initials, J. F., clearly seen. He was a big, buirdly man, but the soul of him is looking out of his fearless eyes even in the photograph. A face of granite, with great lines of strength and dourness about the jaws. Doubtless a man of roaring passions, but a man also of terrific righteousness, who might have cleft the skull of Claverhouse at one stroke, with a prayer to God for his Kirk, his conscience, and his country.

On one occasion, Russel of *The Scotsman* was out shooting at Swanston with a friend. John Todd, who himself was a dead shot, was acting as gamekeeper to them. Both gentlemen had missed a bird, when the Roaring Shepherd took aim with his old gun and brought it down. In those days Todd made his own wads out of bits of newspaper which he carried in his pocket. Russel walked up and looked about him.

" No wonder he killed," said he, " for he's using *The Scotsman* for a wad and a wee bit of the *Courant!* "

A grandson of the Roaring Shepherd told me that he had sometimes seen Stevenson come through the door in the wall at the foot of the garden when John Todd was sorting out the sheep.

" Well, Todd, how are you to-day? "

" I'm no' compleenin'," was the invariable answer of the Roaring Shepherd, for he was a dour philosopher, and grudged affirmatives if a negative would do. Then, when something really went wrong, he let fly a perfect volcano of passion, and there was a fiery stream of lava round the walls of Swanston for the time being. Louis, who was just then learning life, stood listening with a smile of pleasure on his face, for he knew that the eruption would soon subside.

Cummy, with her stiffer religious sense, played counter to the Roaring Shepherd in the life of Louis. For her Sabbatarianism was of the strictest. The shepherd's grandsons used to play with a pony in the paddock at Swanston. But a Sunday circus was forbidden forty years ago. Yet human nature is such that the boys about the farm-town would slip on to the pony's broad back, and have a standing ride round the field when time hung heavy on their hands after the kirk had scaled at Colinton or Glencorse. On one occasion Cummy came down the path with solemn protestations when she saw them at such wickedness.

The boys leaped the wall. But one of them dropped a cap. It was pounced upon by Cummy, and the boy who risked his life and went back for it had to take half an hour of John Calvin's principles from Louis' nurse.

Coming to William Todd's poem, we here have preserved a whole handful of local names at Swanston, which otherwise might have been lost. The Green Craig, the Shearers' Knowes, Toddle Knowes, Routing Hill, Birky Side, the Tailor's Road, Howdens' Hass, Windy Doors, Byreside Nick, Moolypouches, Cock-my-lane, Samson's Stone, the Papples—these were all household words with the villagers of Swanston in Stevenson's day, but some of them we would find it hard to locate now. The old washerwoman referred to was a certain hard worker called Peggy, who did laundry work for Edinburgh families, and bleached her linen on the Swanston Green. Before an important washing she usually consulted the Roaring Shepherd about the weather. Mysie's " gabled wa' " was an old house which stood next door to the shepherd's cottage. It has long ago been demolished.

SWANSTON'S WHINNY KNOWES

Ance mair I tread the whinny knowes
Where gazed the floo'r o' Cheviot yowes,
In childhood days it was my hame
And Honest John the shepherd's name.
I see auld " Snag " and " Cheviot " at his heel
As up the Green Craig he wad spiel,
Ayont the Shearie and the Toddle Knowes
Where aft we buchted a' the yowes.

Noo frae the Green Craig's rocky broo
'Twas his delight his flocks to view;
Here he wad gie the signal to auld " Snag " :
The dowg wi' knowing look his tail wad wag :
Then doon the brae and through the whinny hedge,
Up ower the Routin Hill by cover's edge,
Ower a' the leas wi' lanky stride
He'd turn the sheep aff Birky Side.
Noo John is aff alang the Tailor's Road,
For twa and thirty years by him 'twas trod.
There he takes oot his guid field glass
Views a' the yowes and lambs up Howden's Hass.
Across the brae he takes the sklent
Lampin' ower the wavin' bent,
On tapmost heicht o' Allermair
Breathes in great draughts o' caller air :
Doon Windy Doors and Byreside Nick
Where roon the knowes the rabbits jick,
See foxy slippin' oot o' sicht
Richt ower Kirkyetton's rocky heicht,
While " Cheviot," nicknamed aye the Bear,
Is sniffin' up the tainted air,
His nerves a' quiverin' for the chase
Up steep Kirkyetton's skliddery face
On Moolypouches noo we'll rest
Where aft I've sought the lintie's nest
And even noo I see the auld elm tree
Where built the bonnie blue oxee :
'Twas aye oor brag that tree to sklim
And see the tittie's nest sae trim.
Yonder stands the muckle beech,
Six times roon oor airms did reach :
How loud we made the echoes ring
As on its branches we did swing!
Then doon the windin' whimplin' burn,
Sae weel I ken its every turn :
Till 'mang the whins o Cock-my-lane
Where lies the famous Samson Stane.

Doon its face we went like winkin'
Never on oor coup-carts thinkin':
But up and doon again like winkie
Slid ower the mark o' Samson's pinkie.
But oh the best o' moleskin hide
Could never stand that awfu' slide:
Oor breekies they were seldom hale
And mony a hole showed oor serk tail.
And here's the green, the bonnie green,
Where bairnies played frae morn till e'en,
For washerwives they bleached their claes
Upon its grassy gowaned braes:
While Peggy wad alairm the toon
Cryin' tae some wild wee loon
Wha left the mark o' his bare feet
Upon a braw white linen sheet.
Here at the Pailace we played the bools,
Dod, Dick, and me kenned a' the rules;
Plunk them fu' and nickle deid,
The stunks knocked oot wi' lichtnin speed,
Noo we stand upon the spot
Where aft we played oor game at lot,
Against auld Mysie's gabled wa'
Though aff the plumb and like to fa':
'Twas weel shored up wi' a guid ash tree;
Dod fell ower't and hurt his knee.
Noo behold the auld stane biggin'
Clay-clapped lum and divot riggin',
Mossgrown strae stung on the ruif
Made it wind and water pruif:
But whiles a wind frae the Papples blew
And tirled some theekin' aff the skew:
Inside, the rafters a' were bare
And naething but a yearthen flaer:
It had a but, but no' a ben,
Oh where were a' oor riches then?
Yet weel I mind when I was wee
There kneelin' at my mither's knee,

She taught my lispin' lips to pray
To Him wha made the nicht and day.
Though time rolls on wi' years o' sun and rain,
The laddies still are slidin' doon the Samson Stane.

The last I saw of William Todd that broiling day
was the sturdy old man standing on the hill mutter-
ing poetry to a grandson of the Roaring Shepherd.
A wave of the stick, a shout of " Haste ye back
again," and then a turn of the road hid him from
view. But, as I stepped out, I thought how much
pleasanter it was to hear a sheep-man speaking poetry
on his hills than to hear, as Stevenson must often
have heard, this sheep-man's father sending the
thunder of his wrathful voice like an audible bogie
along the face of Kirkyetton.

XIX

MY WINTER SANCTUARY

THE SPELL OF SOLITUDE

In this century of rush and wonder, tramping is rapidly becoming a lost art. People are looking for short cuts, and shouting themselves hoarse about the right to live, when, all the time, beauty in nooks and corners is eluding these fast livers, who in their very anxiety for life have no time to live. It was that exact and argumentative gentleman called Euclid who taught us that a straight line is the shortest distance between two points—a poor enough way of getting from one place to another, and the direct contradiction of nature, which abhors, not only vacuums, but straight lines. Being no mathematician, the walking man avoids straight lines, broad highways, and obvious tracks. He delights to wander slowly from one place to another, in a happy-go-lucky, zig-zag hunt for those remoter things of life and beauty which the conventional traveller never finds. The true measure of a journey is not how far you have gone, but how much you have seen. So, for all purposes of the eye and ear, it is wiser for the nature lover to walk alone.

This brings me to speak of sanctuaries. A sanctuary means both silence and solitude—the two things which city life has made impossible for the natural man. Yet, to keep his soul in focus every city dweller ought to have some natural sanctuary— a place within easy reach of town, where he is neither teased nor taigled by the crowd, some secret spot where he can bathe his soul in silence, and revel in the sights and sounds of nature.

My winter sanctuary is reached from a little clachan called the Tryst. You step off a bus, and yonder, right fornent you, is a by-road, which, like all true roads, leads you into the heart of the hills. Within a bowshot from the Tryst you come to a solitary kirk, with a war memorial standing in a plot of grass. It is a plain, flat obelisk, made of blocks of the finest sandstone. But the most beautiful thing about this stone to-day is the wonderful colour with which the weathering of a Scots climate in a few years has invested it. The top block bears a bronze wreath. Beneath that, one would think that Turner had painted a series of three impressionistic land-scapes; mere whiffs of colour, that are as delicate as his *Ehrenbreitstein*, or his *Study on the Rhine*. The first is a tranquil river scene, with a faint suggestion of tree-clad banks and the most delicate reflections on the glassy water. The next shows an estuary at sunset with a calm sea, rippling clouds above, little ships suggested on the strip of shining water, with low hills on the horizon. The third is a lonely corrie, with the faintest suggestion of a triple barrier of hills encircling a mist-filled hollow. All this poetry of colour, painted by the weather in sensitive greens and greys, sepias and yellows, on a column of fine sandstone!

At the next turn the natural avenue of the road begins. An old Scots fir stands sentry at the gate on the right, and the road sweeps on and down to a bridge between great trees and straggling beech hedges.

> These hedgerows, hardly hedgerows, little lines
> Of sportive wood run wild.

Beyond the dip you see a conical fir rising from the hollow, and beyond the fir rises the big blue dome of Pentlands' towering top. There is not a more glamorous bit of road near Edinburgh. Stevenson loved it and dreamed of it beyond all others. I have travelled it in every season and in every month of the year. Yet I like it best in winter-time, for the trees are more friendly when they are bare, and the colours of winter are so delicate and soft that they more than compensate for all those gloomy days which make a mood of melancholy in the soul.

On the bridge itself the stones are green with moss splashed with bright yellow ochres. The stream whispers beneath, with a weird murmur of reminiscence which brings back the voice of the exiled Scot in Samoa ettling after home—" I shall never take that walk . . . I shall never see Auld Reekie. I shall never set my foot again on the heather . . . Do you know where the road crosses the burn . . . ? Go there and say a prayer for me—*moriturus salutat*. See that it is a sunny day . . . Shut your eyes, and if I don't appear to you! " Surely his spirit haunts this place to-day and meets

all who come to the ruined kirk up-by.[1]   There
are some places where one has been so often that
there is no accounting of the visits now.   So is this
most romantic old kirkyard by far the dearest to me
of all the kirkyards round Edinburgh.   I know it
when the snows of winter lie upon it like a dazzling
winding sheet, with the dead streikit under its
spotless folds in awful silence: when the summer
sunshine floods its well-bielded graves with a warm
radiance, and when yon banks of rhododendrons
beyond the furthest field blaze red and pink and
white in the evening afterglow, and the rabbits come
out to gambol in the gloaming.   Here the first
snowdrops whiten the green graves, and the ruined
kirk with its ivy-covered walls and wooden spire
looks as if it were a thousand years old.

How many old folks and young folks were carried
up the stey brae from the bend of the road to be
laid in the old God's Acre!   Yon worn step at the
gate is eloquent of the myriad feet that have come
here to worship or to mourn, and woe to that man
who tries to even that deep dented stone.[2]   For, from
the brae to the wooden steeple of the ruined kirk
among the tree-encircled graves, the whole scene is
a perfect poem of man's mortality.

It is good-bye now to roads until we reach the
sanctuary.   A vault over a gate brings you, in the
early months of winter into a cow pasture and
there is nothing which adds such a tranquil sense of
life to a landscape of woodlands and meadows like a

[1] If this is not the place " where the road crosses the burn "
it will be found beyond the church where the road from the
manse crosses the Glencorse Burn.
[2] The steps are now protected.

lot of clean, brown-and-white cows. A whiff of milk
is in the air, and the sound of browsing beasts adds
a sense of company in the quiet meadow. At the
further side there is another gate, and a step across
the muddy lane leads to a strip of woodland. This
is the beginning of a paradise of woods beyond.
You can hear the tooting of a south-going motor
on the road. But here, in the deeps of the wood,
with a carpet of red leaves for the feet, and the great
beeches and pines swaying almost imperceptibly in
the breeze, we are far removed from company. The
pheasants and the cushats flutter in the dark green
cover above. In that dense thicket of little spruces
I once saw a couple of roe-deer flitting out of their
cover with oriflammes all aglow in the wintry gloaming—the nearest place to Edinburgh where I have
ever startled these fairy phantoms of the woods.
Down on the right the little stream which we are
to follow to its source bubbles and flows along the
edge of the wood. Here and there on the waterside you will find tidy little bundles of firewood
lying at the foot of a great fir tree, besides the tell-
tale ashes of an old fire—the unmistakable signs
that the stravaiger has been there, and has left
material for future bliss. It is a heartsome place,
with the sweet scent of pine trees and the good
wholesome tang of wet earth and leaf-mould, the
constant sound of running water, and the great
hills making a blue background beyond the bare
trees. A step over the wall on to the tar-sprayed
highway and a plunge into the wood on the other
side takes us still further up this delightsome woodland stream, until the open amphitheatre of a green

meadow brings us to the very gateway of the hills. There they are, rising steep on every side, like sleeping lions with tawny shoulders and shaggy manes.

Here by this grassy waterside, on a certain day of every week, you will meet a man and a dog coming down from the ravine of the pine trees to look the water at the same hour, and all through the months of winter this is the only company. Yonder is a heron flapping its heavy wings over the tree tops to its haunt in the valley beyond the loch. All day in the woods and in the hedgerows the great tit has been sounding his double note, like the sound of a melodious saw. I never hear this bird but I think of the ever-recurring motif in one of the movements of Tchaikovsky's Symphony in E minor. Surely Tchaikovsky must have heard this musical woodsaw, as the bird is called, in the woods of Russia before he reproduced the call so exactly, and made the notes such a striking feature in the movement of this Symphony.

But the sounds of nature to-day are as nothing to the colour of nature. See yon bright purple mist! It is a great hawthorn, ablaze with a wealth of red haws. Here is another, and another, making little splashes of glowing colour in the bosky deeps of the ravine. Another corner turned, and the surprise of the gorge bursts on us—a snow-white waterfall, tumbling down a craggy height among the pines. So carefully hidden from all roads is this secret ravine, that it was many years before I caught a glimpse of the waterfall from high up on the hill. A step over a wooden bridge brings us

N

to the other side of the stream, and the last stage of the journey is reached. Here you can find shelter on the wildest day among the solemn pine trees, which stand motionless while the gale roars in their throats far up. For while the little ash saplings and the willows rive and struggle and protest in the teeth of the wind, the pine trees stand like dreaming giants whose immemorial peace nothing can disturb.

The path ends at last at a steep, grassy bank. When you reach the top with a pech, after speiling the stiff slope, the loch stretches before you in all its tranquil beauty, with an island in the middle distance and rolling hills on every side. Take the sheep track to the left, and after creeping round a pine-clad bluff above the water, in another moment you are down in the sanctuary—a green hollow, scooped out of the hillside above the loch, with one or two pine trees, and the bracken-clad hills rising up and up until their rounded summits meet the blue.

At the foot of a pine tree in the sanctuary you will find lying, all through the winter, a neat pile of fire faggots, with a bundle of feathery twigs. Close to the tree is the ash foundation of the last fire. Sometimes the day is quiet and lown. Sometimes it is cold and clear, with a bite of north in the wind. Sometimes the grass is white with frost. But soon the twigs are lit, the faggots feed the flame, and a roaring pine fire makes the coldest winter day warm. The rucksack is unpacked, the pungent smell of reek is equalled only by the fragrance of the finest coffee in the world, and lying there by the blazing fire, with a faggot for a pipelight, and the little waves lapping peacefully on the rocks below, I find my winter sanctuary far from a busy world. Here none can disturb the longest dreams, for the only company is a flock of wild ducks that sail out and in, with an occasional splutter and quack, from the ferny shores of the loch. Many a time in the busy streets the thought of it comes to my mind. Then I smell the pines and feel the hill-breeze on the cheek, and forgetting the city's noise, I live for a moment in the tranquil peace of the sanctuary. Also I murmur to myself this sentiment of a mystic Celt, W. B. Yeats: —

And I shall have some peace there, for peace comes
         dropping slow,
    Dropping from the veils of the morning to where the
         cricket sings;
There midnight's all a-glimmer, and noon a purple
         glow,
    And evening full of the linnet's wings.

I will arise and go now, for always night and day
    I hear lake water lapping with low sounds by the
         shore;
While I stand on the roadway, or on the pavements
         gray,
    I hear it in the deep heart's core.

XX

WINTER WANDERINGS IN WEST LOTHIAN

I

IT is a common belief of the city-bred man that summer is the only time for country walks. For, in our adventurous climate, we are all more or less afraid of the weather. But to the wandering man, winter beauty is as fascinating as summer beauty, and only those who know the world of woodlands, fields, and open roads, all the year round, can ever enter into the secret of nature's charms. And yet it is such an obvious loss to so many dwellers in our romantic city of Edinburgh, that they never seem to explore the by-ways of wonder which lie just beyond our own backdoors. East, south, or west, wherever you wander it is the same—a land comfortable with little Lothian townships that send up the smoke of bein industries; a land steeped in the lore of ancient places and peoples that are forgotten in the rush of a more pushful age. The true gangrel scorns all means of travel but his own feet. But I care not whether you walk or cycle or use a motor car to help you out between the exploits—if you come with me on this mellow winter morning, you will be glad that you can claim to be a Lothian man.

THE CARMELITE CHAPEL, SOUTH QUEENSFERRY

Let us begin our real stravaig at Queensferry—
that fascinating spot which brings up the ghosts
of old Scots romance; from Margaret, Queen of
Malcolm Canmore, the finest royal lady who ever
sat on a Scots throne, to douce David Balfour of
The Shaws, who interviewed that consummate sea-
dog, Elias Hoseason, in a little upstairs room of the
old Hawes Inn.   Queensferry itself is associated in
the minds of most Edinburgh folks with the Forth
Bridge, the British Fleet, trippers, and char-a-bancs.
But to-day as we walk along the narrow street, we
pause before a very ancient building on the right
hand, and enter the open door.   It is all that remains
of the monastery of the Carmelite Friars, who got
a charter from Dundas of Dundas in 1457 to build
this modest House of God—but, there is a sough in
history of a church here as early as 1330.   So few
people know about the old-world repose of this
ancient chapel—yet, you have only to step inside and
the cloistered gloom of centuries falls upon you.
The austere simplicities of this old monastery take
you worlds away from the clatter of the street.   It
was restored in 1890, and since that time has been
used as an Episcopalian Chapel.   In the choir, the
sedila, the piscina, and the ambry are all there, and
a little transcept is built out to the south.   It is a
plain aisleless church, a hundred feet long, with bare
stone walls and a vaulted roof.   We have a long road
to travel and must be going but it is hard to leave
the dreams of ancient peace which rise within us, as
we pass out again into the winter sunshine.   Look
up at the square tower.   It was originally finished
with the cape house and parapet walk which were

so common in Scots architecture of the fifteenth
century. In that tower the friars lived comfortably
for two hundred years, toasting their toes on the cold
days at the open fireplaces after climbing the wheel-
stair. Before our day's wanderings are over we shall
see another ancient tower of the same style. But ere
passing on, it is well worth while looking at the rocks
on the shoreward side of the monastery, for the
monks are said to have chiselled out a harbour, with
their own hands. If the tide is out you have only
to step behind the monastery, cross a wide green,
and drop on to the shore. Then a rather sludgy
walk down the beach will show you a solid pier of
natural rock, sheered down doubtless by the monks'
chisels into the wall of a long jetty—for these
ancient friars were expert workers in all the ordinary
arts.

Step westward now, and the modern ugliness of
Queensferry will be forgotten in your glamorous
thoughts of the past. For thus it is, that a sense of
ancient beauties helps us often to pass with good
humour through many modern barbarisms.

We have to take the high road now, as Port Edgar
is a naval base. But all our interest in Port Edgar
to-day is, that the very name reminds us of Queen
Margaret's brother. Afar cry indeed, from the
primitive ship which anchored out yonder in the
year 1068 with the beautiful Princess on board, to
this naval base whose secrets none of us dare know!
The road, which now runs by the sea, past the stately
entrance gates to Hopetoun House—these gates
which open of their own accord, like the prison
gate in Scripture—is a bit of quite unspoiled shore

scenery. On a sunny winter morning the views up and down and across the Forth are full of a quiet, elusive beauty. Here is a group of picturesque, high-built houses, with gardens behind and a flat green by the sea and a turreted corner house with a little policy all its own—it is called by the quaint name of Society. Something in its old-farrant atmosphere and stance reminds us irresistibly of Robert Louis Stevenson, who could surely have cast great glamour over this same Society, if only he had peopled these bald Scots houses by the green with a handful of cut-throat adventurers; adding a cosy change-house with a settle by the fire; and one of Nelson's jolly old sea captains, with a wooden leg, in the mysterious corner house, whose windows are continually winking in the sun.

The way now leads us up an avenue of ancient trees to Hopetoun House, that grey palace which stands with such a noble frontage, amid great lawns. If you are motoring, send your car round by the public road, past the gardens and the Blue Gate, to meet you at Abercorn, or better still at Blackness, and come with me on one of the most delectable of walks. Up the narrow dark avenue we pass, with the great trees meeting overhead, the grey palace standing on the right. Turning north at the corner we come on one of these delightful tricks of land-scape gardening—a circular pond let into the lawn, as a mirror to reflect most beautifully the great house standing beyond the splendid sweep of greensward.

Following the path, which skirts a sunny little valley with a pleasant prospect to the west, we pass through the winter woods to the Bastion Walk over-

looking the Forth—a straight walk, high up above
the deer park, which runs along the shore. The
seaward side of the walk is lined with a thick unbroken yew hedge, with circular bastions here and
there which are themselves lined with very old yew.
The view westward is wide and beautiful, past
Blackness Castle to the upper reaches of the Forth
by Stirling, eastward to the mighty bridge and the
outgate of the North Sea beyond, and across to the
couthie Fife shores and busy Rosyth. It is all so
quiet and remote and fair, with the winter woodlands behind, the wide waters in front, and down
below, a great stag bellowing with his antlered head
outstretched. Yonder he wanders in his winter coat,
reminding us of his fellows who have more need
than he to fight their neighbours in the lonely glens
among the Highland hills. So still can it be here
that on a misty winter day I have stood in this bastion
and located the deer by the sound of a dozen of them
nibbling the grass. Near this spot stood the ancient
castle of Abercorn, the strongest of the three local
castles of the Douglas Clan—Inveravon, Blackness,
and Abercorn. The castle was reduced after a
month's siege in the year 1455, and nothing of it
stands to-day but a circular mound marking its site.
All trace of the building was removed when the
modern grounds of Hopetoun were laid out. To-day
we stand dreaming of the downfall of the Douglases
—a fell family for centuries in our land. But now,
in this countryside, nothing of their glory remains.

At the end of the Bastion Walk there is a locked
gate—but most wonders in this world lie just beyond
barred gates. So, if you are a true stravaiger, a

leap will find you on the other side, standing by an old sundial, with a hope in your heart that you may be forgiven. You are now gazing down into one of the sweetest spots on the Lothian shore—a deep Devon-like coomb, with a stream singing its way between woody banks down to the creek and a grey old house in a garden, sending up blue reek from the very depths of the dell. The old church of Abercorn just hints at its own presence above the tree-fringed height on the landward side of the cove, and the red-deer are belling in the park below. Leap another gate and you are following the old road to the shore, past the house in the hollow. To-day the tide is out, and the sea birds are calling continually from the edge of the water. A solitary whaup is trying its whistle, and now and again the oystercatchers call. Sitting here on the crumbling sea-wall, with the gluck of little waves at the feet, freits of fancy spring up in the mind and people this silent cove with children of romance—old days, the clash of arms in the sun, secret ongoings of smugglers on the dark nights, a low whistle in the pitchy woods (or was it only a hoolet?), and the sound of muffled oars out there at the mouth of the burn!

This coomb of Abercorn is threaded by two burns, which join one another just above a grey stone bridge. The tiny rivulet which comes from the south-east, and which doubtless was a larger stream a thousand years ago, is called the Cornie Burn; the other, and much larger one, which comes from the south-west, is the Pardovan or Midhope Burn. The Church in ancient days seems always to have sat cheek-by-jowl with the queerest uncos of blood

and witchery. So the church of Abercorn up yonder
has for over a thousand years kept its eye on the
secret ploys of the adventurers in this hollow coomb.
Once upon a time, long gone by, the kingdom of
Northumbria came as far as this very spot, and St
Wilfred founded a cell here in the year 675 at
Aebbercurnig or Abercornie, which means the mouth
of the Cornie Burn. Under Trumwin, this church
became the See of the earliest bishopric in Scotland.
But when the Picts defeated the Northumbrians at
Dunichen, the monks of Abercorn fled to Whitby,
and on the site of this earliest church the later ones
were built. The present church incorporates a fine
old Norman doorway, with nook shafts, cushion caps,
and a tympanum which is filled in with stones
arranged in zigzag fashion. It is worth coming up
the dell to this old kirk of Abercorn to see the
ancient doorway, the two carved stones at the back
of the church—one of them part of an old cross, and
a hog-backed stone in the churchyard—and to admire
the peaceful tree-embowered clachan, with its trim
houses and fine manse.

Avoiding the main road, we resume our wanderings down at the old grey bridge by the sea-mouth
of the coomb, for we are yet to meet surprise after
surprise of romance and beauty in these Lothian
by-ways. Instead of scrambling along the shore to
blackness we take a most unexpected woodland walk
up the Pardovan or Midhope stream, which leads
through mellow winter glades, all russet and gold
and brown. Crossing and recrossing the stream by
two rustic bridges, past an old moss-grown stone-
covered fountain amid the groves, then by an old-

world sawmill, and finally emerging from the woods, we are surprised by the tall entrance gates of a forsaken mansion, just where the path ends at a bridge across the mill dam. Into this bridge is built the remains of an old cross. Passing this outer gate, we walk up to the great inner gate of Midhope Castle, noting a fine example of a dovecot on the left.

The castle is a gaunt Scots keep, with its westmost roof towering against the sky. The courtyard is approached through a massive stone archway, with three spherical finials atop, and an old carved stone let into the right wall—A.D.1582.MB. Within the gateway silence reigns, but for a few ruminating hens; and the only sign of habitation in the castle is the suggestion of a curtain in a window here and there. This was once the country house of the Livingstons, the old-time Earls of Linlithgow, whose town residence was within the Royal Palace of Linlithgow. One of their progenitors—Trustan Leving—witnessed a legal deed of gift for William de Lindsay of Binny, who granted a piece of ground to the chapel of St Giles of Binny as far back as 1187. Here you may still see, over the castle door, a coronet and the initials J L. But some stones of the old house of the Drummonds, onetime owners of Midhope, have been built into the walls—which accounts for the AD. on the stone we have just seen on the inner gateway. Another of these stones, at the right hand side of the main door, is very worn now; but it bears the pious inscription in black-letter carving, which is difficult to read now: *Tangene Depres Jesus*—Touch not the thorns of Jesus. Such

French inscriptions were common on old Scots houses of the time of James VI. The green courtyard in front of the high Scots castle with its crow-stepped gables; a few cottages outside the archway and across the grassy yard; an old garden with two ancient yew trees—what an old-world tang of reminiscence hangs round Midhope this winter day!

The yew trees are of great girth—one of them thirteen feet, the other fourteen feet, and in the early summer a carpet of blue periwinkles is spread beneath. It was told me long ago, when first I wandered here, that these two trees mark the burial place of two Covenanters. For did not many an outed fugitive of faith fly from that old man-hunter, Tam Dalyell of The Binns, yonder? Did not that namely minister, John Blackadder of Troqueer, preach often in this countryside? And was not good Donald Cargill himself spied upon by John Pairk, the worthless minister of Borrowstounness, as he was sauntering along the shore down-by? These and many other old tales we think upon as we sit watching the pigeons preening themselves on the pete stones of the high gables in the wan sunlight of this strangely lown winter day.

A mile and a half, still westward we go, across the high open fields, with fine views of the Highland hills and the upper waters of the Forth, to yon grim fortress standing bluff and square on a promontory—Blackness Castle. The tower on the rising ground to the left marks the estate of a once notorious man—General Sir Thomas Dalyell of The Binns. Blackness and Binns—how these two names have been thirled in Scottish history to many a black deed!

It was this same Tam Dalyell who raised the Scots Greys and used them to hunt down the Covenanters. He learned all his barbarisms in Russia. But to the Tartars he brought a heart that was not ill to teach —for when he came back to Scotland he was called the Muscovy Brute. He never shaved his beard after the execution of his royal master, Charles I. His favourite game at Binns was hell—so the old word goes. For, after a hearty meal and a heartier drink, he would lock himself and his guests in a room with a whip apiece, and there they lashed and cursed each other in the dark, until the devil took the side of the hindmost drunken reveller who could stand. He put old women and children to the torture, and would kill old men by slow degrees in loathesome dungeons. Binns, up yonder, was his den—Blackness down here was his dungeon. In those bad days, no bairn in Scotland durst laugh at Tam Dalyell of The Binns. So, we shake our fists at the tower and pass through the long-shore woods to the sands beneath this Covenanter prison, which will for ever be mentioned in history with that other State prison of dark memories—the Bass.

Blackness was the ancient seaport of Linlithgow, until in 1680, Borrowstounness, a few miles further up the shore, took its place. But this grim old castle would take a whole history book to tell its story—a story which begins with the end of that old song the Roman occupation. The Black Douglas lords, Scots kings and queens, raids and burnings, State prisoners, English bombardments, Cromwell and his soldiers, Covenanters and Conventiclers—

they all took a hand in making history here on its battlements and in its dungeons. Up on the green tuft of the castle hill you can still trace the remains of St Ninian's Chapel. But Blackness stands far up the Forth, now a grim relic of the days that were.

XXI

WINTER WANDERINGS IN WEST LOTHIAN

II

IF the car which you left at Hopetoun has taken the right road, it should be standing waiting for you at the castle gate as you come off the green turf of the little hill. Driving along the quiet, pleasant by-ways by Champany and Bonnytoun, three miles and a bittock will bring you into the old world town of Linlithgow. To any Scot with a taste for history in his soul Linlithgow, with its Palace and its Parish Kirk on the height overlooking the loch, is a hard town to pass through, tempting him as it does to linger for the rest of the day around this noble burgh town, with its Royal Palace of the Stuart Kings. But all the world knows Linlithgow, and our wanderings to-day are to take us among the unexplored by-ways of the country. So, passing slowly along the High Street to the west end, we take the road due south, across the canal, and breast the braes for a couple of miles. On the right lie the policies of Preston House; a swing round the steep bit of road with the nasty turn called the devil's elbow, and we halt at the summit, where the road skirts the base of that miniature West Lothian mountain—Cockleroy.

If it is a clear day, it will repay anyone to walk to the top of Cockleroy (912 feet) to get one of the finest views in the Lothians—westward to the Grampians, north to the Ochils, east to the lands of home about Auld Reekie, and south to the quiet green hills round Torphichen, which we are now to explore. Fife, Clackmannan, Perth, Stirling, Dumbarton, Lanark, Linlithgow, Midlothian, and Haddington—these nine shires, at least, are plainly visible on this clear winter day from Cock-le-roi, the Hill of Kings. The name of William Wallace is in the very air of the place. Yonder on the River Avon is Wallace's cave. At Torphichen, over there, Wallace issued mandates in the year 1298. Here where we stand on this hill-top is Wallace's bed, and over at Polmont is a village called Wallacetown.

Standing on Cockleroy one recalls Robert Louis Stevenson's lines in his poem, "The Scotsman's Return from Abroad"—

> In mony a foreign pairt I've been
> And mony an unco ferlie seen,
> Since, Mr Johnstone, you and I
> Last walkit upon Cocklerye.
>
> . . . . .
>
> Wi whatna joy I hailed them a',
> The hilltaps standin' raw by raw,
> The public-house, the Hielan' birks,
> And a' the bonny U.P. Kirks!

—which shows us that Stevenson must have looked on this unrivalled Lothian view, with its panorama of Highland hills in the far distance—Ben Lomond, Stobinian, Ben More, Stuc-a-Chroin, Ben Voirlich, Ben Ledi, and Dumyat—and afterwards poked his robustious fun at the barnlike kirks of the douce secession burghers in the sleepy town down by.

Just below the hill, on the south side, you can see an old ruined castle in a farmyard. That is Kipps Castle, once the property and residence of Sir Robert Sibbald, physician to Charles II., and an early historian of the county. Near the castle you can see also the remains of an ancient Celtic cromlech, which stood within a circle of stones. Now descend to the road and continue a little way due south. It is a very quiet, remote countryside, which is best known to members of the Linlithgowshire Fox Hunt and to stravaigers like ourselves. For that very reason, few city dwellers know the treasures of ancient things which lie in the heart of these green hills. Yet, here, we are to come to the greatest adventure of the day—for, even now, we are treading the once sacred ground of a city of refuge. The chivalrous Knights of St John of Jerusalem erected this refuge garth 850 years ago, with their monastery at Torphichen as a centre, and certain grey old stones to mark the holy circle which claimed the country within a radius of one mile as sanctuary. On five of these sanctuary stones we may actually lay our hands to-day.

On Craigmailing Hill, on the left hand side of the road, a little further on than Kipps Castle, there is a wooded height called the Witches' Craig. Climb this, and when you get to the top of the wood you will find a wall with a hunt gate in it opening on to the turf beyond. Built into the wall, on the south side of the gate, there is a great stone set in the coping with a double-branched cross

o

carved in relief on its face. Pass through the gate, and you will see another cross deeply incised on the other side of the stone. This is one of the only remaining refuge stones which made the circle of sanctuary for one mile round the ancient church of the Knights of St John of Jerusalem. Their church still stands in ruins alongside of the Parish Church of Torphichen, behind yon little green hills. These Knight-Hospitallers came to Linlithgowshire in the year 1124, and built their priory with the consent of King David I. of Scotland—that " sair sanct for the croon " and great cathedral builder, who would have welcomed a monk in any guise. The Torphichen Priory, in common with other monasteries, possessed the right of sanctuary. All criminals, debtors, and accused persons who could outrace their pursuers and reach one of these refuge stones were safe from molestation. They were then within the circle of mercy. Thereafter, they were sure of finding justice at the hands of the Knights of St. John. Only four of these boundary stones remain standing to-day— this cross-carved Craigmailing stone to the eastward of the monastery; another in a little wood-enclosed field on the side of the avenue to Lochcote House, to the north; a third lying half-buried in a wood near Westfield Paper Mills, to the west; and the fourth standing in a field near Causton, on the south, about two miles from Bathgate. The ordnance map marks one in a field below Craigmailing Hill, beyond the ruins of the little farm called Haddies Walls, but this stone is well within the mile circle. Easy to locate when directed to them, these stones cost the writer many a hunt and tramp ere he found them all.

The Craigmailing stone is the only one of special interest from a sketching point of view on account of its remarkable crosses. Place your hand on it, close your eyes, and let your imagination work. You will almost hear the gasp of relief on this silence-encircled hill as some blood-stained transgressor falls exhausted, with his fingers clutching the Refuge Stone. The centuries crumble away, and you see a Knight of Christ approach the penitent on this hallowed spot.

Before leaving Craigmailing Hill, step over the turf to the east side of the hill and you will find near a wall the Preaching Stone, as it is called. It is a plain, dour, weather-beaten boulder embedded deeply in the hillside, framed in gorse, and graven with a clean-cut inscription, which tells the passer-by that on this spot Mr John Hunter preached from a certain text on the second Sabbath of January 1738. We do not grudge breaking in for a moment on our memories of the old monkish hospitallers of St John to mark this spot, where, in the later centuries, the hardy Seceders with plaid and staff first gathered to worship God, from Falkirk, Shotts, Lanark, the Calders, and Queensferry. For thus the inscription runs: " Jany. 14th, 1738. Here was pred. ye 1st Sern. by ye most worthy Mr Hunter, from ye 37th Chapr. of Ezek. and ye 26th Verse "; and below is added the date 1732, which is the year of the first secession.

A stone's-throw further south, and you join a side road which leads to Torphichen, at the little farm-place of Lower Craigmailing. Part of the walls of this farm belonged to the great barn-like kirk which

latterly was used by the Seceders. Here, by the side
of a little window, you can still see the foundation-
stone with its chiselled inscription below the white-
wash: " Founded May 1742." I knew a man whose
grandmother was carted or carried as a little babe
from Carnwath to Craigmailing for baptism—sixteen
miles as the crow flies, and a good twenty by road.
Siccar saints were these old Seceders.

The winter day is now drawing to its dusk, so
we take the road again, from Lower Craigmailing,
past Cathlaw House, to Torphichen. Passing through
the village, with its quaint up-and-down streets, we
enter the old kirkyard to visit the priory, or the
Quhair (choir), as it is still called. It stands in
stately ruins, with a bald, ugly kirk of late date
built on to it. As you go up the path from the gate,
between the graves, you will see a little square
stone, like a milestone, standing in the turf, on the
left-hand side. Here is the stone which was the
very centre of the circle of sanctuary. It is unique.
On the top of it you will find a cross and a small
holy water font or cup which, doubtless, the earliest
monks of Christ carved on it. But, look down one
of the flat sides, and you will also see five strangely
smooth little cup markings. That, to the antiquary's
eye, is the most interesting sight in this whole day's
wanderings. For cup markings make one of the
mysteries of archæology. The wise man will not
dogmatise about their meaning. He will only say
that these little cups or hollows are to be found on
stones in Britain, Scandinavia, France, Germany,
and Switzerland, and that they point to some superstitious kind of worship which survived in the late

TORPHICHEN QUHAIR

Iron Age, or even in a modified form to Christain times.

Take, then, this cup-marked stone in the old kirk-yard of Torphichen, and if you can imagine it as some mysterious pagan altar-stone, which once lay flat with its little cups running full, what a wonderful vision rises before the mind! The monks of Christ arrive. They find this pagan altar-stone, lying where our pre-Christian ancestors left it on this magic-haunted worship-spot. They raise it on its end, carve upon its top the sign of the Cross, and hollow out the font and set about converting the pagans to Christianity. There you see one of the most interesting ecclesiastical records in Scotland; a single stone, showing by its markings, religion redeeming superstition; Christianity replacing paganism, the Holy Cross set above the cup mark! There may be other stones in Scotland of a similar kind—I have heard of one in Aberdeenshire with the Cross and the cup on it—but I know of no other which combines cup, Cross, and holy water font.

One glance at the outside of the Quhair will show you the same castle-like tower and cape roof which we noticed in the morning at Queensferry. There remains nothing now but the tower and the two short transepts with a complete dwelling-place over each, thus hinting at a row of dormitories which may have occupied an upper floor. If you are fortunate enough to get hold of the key, step inside, and you will see a fine vaulted roof—the recess of the tomb where once lay the effigy of Sir Walter Lindsay, the last preceptor but one, of Torphichen Quhair (1538) —and a piscina alongside with a neatly constructed square basin. The memories of eight centuries grip up in the gloom and silence of this vaulted church.

Outside, the winter sun is setting. The sound of the village children at play comes to us through the twilight. There is scarcely light enough to notice the two serpent-and-apple stones in the kirkyard. But we have seen enough for one winter day to make us realise that just beyond the doors of home, there is a glamorous world of old romance if only we will leave the highway and take to the by-ways. Bathgate is just two miles away. That modern blessing to poor tramps—the motor bus— will take us all the way home to the city for a trifle, if we be so minded. But travel one way or another, we will have seen enough in our winter wanderings through West Lothian to convince us that the by-paths just beyond the city boundaries are steeped in history and romance.

XXII

CASTLE EERIE

MYSTERY, like a vapour, hangs about old houses, and the very essence of mystery is a ghost. We never associate ghosts with sunshine and flowers. The fairies always hold their revels on the mid-summer nights. Fairies are so young and happy. But, ghosts are deathly things. They smell of the grave. They send trickles of fear through our souls. They are of the order of spirits that walk abroad on the winter nights when darkness and silence brood over the hinmost days of the year. They love the small hours before the dawn, and move along the creaking corridors or up the rickety stairs of many an old house, which stands among its immemorial trees, where the hoolets hoot in the moonlight, and the white beams steal through the little old windows of an ancient hall.

If you wish to find the haunted house, you must leave the city and wander out to the edge of the civic bounds, where the houses threaten to obliterate the ancient landmarks, and the smoke-stacks of an industrial age blacken the last of the fine old trees. Take the shore road from Granton to Cramond,

and before you have gone very far you will notice
on your left a pair of tall quaint stone pillars with
a rough wooden gate between them, standing in the
dull December twilight.   Here is an ideal entry to
the world of eerie.   Ichabod is written over the
whole place, and the sea waves on the desolate shore
behind you seem to be sighing with regret for the
Dukes and Lords and gentrice who once passed
between these pillars, and will never pass again.
As you step through a side door you will doubtless
wonder where the fine wrought-iron gates are that
once adorned these stately pillars with the ducal
coronets surmounting their carved finials. You might
still lay your hands upon them if you seek them out
by Gogar, but there will be a grudge in your heart
against the well-known judge who removed them
about a hundred years ago.

Pass up the trim walk, which runs beside a trick-
ling stream between the seagate and the old house,
anl you will find yourself trying to resolve this
droll conundrum of sentiment—whether you are
chapping at the yett of a seventeenth-century laird
or seeking orders at the office of the business firm
that now occupies this precious old mansion, and
preserves its treasure so well.

You would need a good pair of eyes to read the
Latin inscription on the square tablet which is built
into he balustrade high up above the front door.
But here we have a clue to the building of this
" cottage " or *turguriolum,* as this double mansion
was originally meant to be.   For the sake of a
degenerate age which no longer thinks and writes
in Latin, I beg leave to transliterate this singular

memorial. Indeed, it might very well pass for a morality in these times: —

> Riches unemployed are of no avail; but when passed round do much good. Increase of gear means increase of care. Wherefore, for their own comfort and that of their friends, George and Anne, Viscount and Viscountess of Tarbat, have caused this small cottage (*turguriolum*) to be built in the year of the Christian era, 1685. Enter then, O guest, for this is the house of entertainment. It is ours now : soon it will be another's : but whose afterwards we neither know nor care. For none hath a certain dwelling. Therefore, let us live while we may.

As I was standing in the gloaming turning over the beauty of this quaint memorial a voice seemed to whisper from the great bush near by—

" Whase aught this hoose? "

But a man in search of ghosts is not likely to let himself be taigled with genealogies or leaseholds. Let us suffice to say that George Mackenzie, Viscount Tarbat and first Earl of Cromarty, built this place of Royston; that John, second Duke of Argyle, the good Duke of Jeanie Deans, bought it and rechristened it Caroline Park after his queen: and that, when the Duke's daughter married the Earl of Dalkeith, the estate passed to the Duke of Buccleuch, in whose family the house remained until a few years ago. This dateless rigmarole of lairdship might be easily exalted into a whole history which began with Charles II. and ended with Victoria of blessed memory—but our only object is to win at the last resident, who was no other than that siccar

old Scots songstress, Lady John Scott of Spottis-
woode, whose whole life was expressed in her
favourite motto—" Haud fast by the past." She
has left a glamerie about this old house, not to speak
of a green ghost, and the mysterious sound of a
bumping cannon ball in the " Aurora " drawing-
room. So let us slip in at the front door ere the
light of this December day is quite gone, and tread
softly from room to room.

It is a queer double-fronted mansion. For his
lordship who bigged it, in 1685, was not for long
contented with a cottage. He transformed his
turguriolum into a regular mansion, built the new
house round a hollow court, changed the main
entrance from the north side to the south side, so
that to-day you will find a flagged path across the
courtyard, from the one door to the other, with a
covering roof running all the way. The feature of
the newer south front is the pair of canopied roofs
at either end, giving the place the character of an
old French château. As you go up the main stairway you will not move very fast, so interested will
you be in the wrought-iron balustrade of flowers
and arabesques; while in that on the lesser stairway you will admire the cunning artistry that has
interwoven in metal, the thistle, the rose, and the
oak leaf. One reception room has a fine plaster
ornament on the roof, like a circular frame, enclosing
an oil painting of Aurora, or the Dawn, by N. Heude,
Inventor. In the next room the ceiling is equally
fine, with a painting of Diana and Endymion by the
same artist. There are monochromes on the walls
of several rooms which are believed to have been

painted by De la Cour, an artist who did similar work in some Edinburgh houses. In an upstairs lumber room there is a priest's hidie-hole, with a secret passage behind the wall, an ill place to perambulate to-day for a man who wears anything but a gangrel's duds. A gey place is the coal-house at the left-hand side of the north door, downstairs. It was the larder, and the great iron hooks from which the oxen were hung are still fixed in the vaulted roofs. On the floor there is an opening which leads to the old wine cellars.

But to me the mystery of the whole place is to be found in the Aurora drawing-room. I can see Lady John Scott sitting in this white panelled room, with the portraits of the exiled Stuart kings all about her, playing her harp and singing the immortal songs which she wrote and composed: " Ettrick," " Duris-deer "—and many another, and by the touch of her genius transforming " Annie Laurie " into one of our finest songs. It was but yesterday in an older mansion than this that I met one, who said that to have heard Lady John sing " Annie Laurie " to her own accompaniment on the harp, was to lose something each time the song is sung by anyone else.

It was about eleven o'clock one night that the unearthly sound was heard. The limpid notes of the harp and singer's sweet voice were silent and Lady John was sitting all alone. The night was as still as death. Suddenly, the window was burst open and a cannon ball came bounding into the room, bumping its way across the floor with three resounding thumps, until it lay at the foot of a draught screen. Lady John rang the bell furiously, but when the servants appeared the window was closed, there was no sign of any damage, and the ball could not be found. As there are no rooms above the Aurora drawing-room, the mystery was never explained. But in 1879 a governess witnessed the same performance, heard the same sound, and was so terrified that she would never again sit alone in the room. Indeed, the cannon ball episode became so usual in Caroline Park that the two family servants who were always left in charge of the house, grew quite accustomed to it, and ceased to be even alarmed. Here surely was a freit that was more than mere fancy!

At the east side of the house, under the trees where the daffodils used to blow, there was in Lady John's day an old moss-grown well; and in the little square courtyard of the house there hung an alarm bell. Her grand-nieces, who often stayed with her, would not have gone near that well for worlds, in the dark of a winter night, not for fear of tumbling into it, but for fear of what might come out of it. For at midnight the green ghost of a former Lady Royston used to rise slowly out of the well, and walk in her mystic robes of emerald across the field to the front door. How she passed through the steikit yett I know not, but she next appeared in the courtyard and rang the alarm bell. Did not Lady John's grand-niece, Margaret Warrender, many a time lie abed and listen to the tolling of the bell when everybody was asleep in the old house, and the night was still, with not a breath of wind to sway the iron tongue? Standing under the covered way in the courtyard on this dark December day I

THE OLD SEA-GATE OF CAROLINE PARK

looked for the bell, but it was gone. What would we not give if at midnight we could creep in here and see the Green Lady flitting, distraught, along the covered way, making search for the old bell rope!

It was an eerie Jacobite atmosphere that hung about Royston in those days, when old Scrymgeour, the last family gardener, used to work among the enchanting tangle of flowers, fruit trees, and shady bowers that made the garden. The old walled garden is there still, with the ruins of Royston Castle at the north-west angle of the wall. Peaches and apricots ripened on the walls in those delicious days. Surely the suns must have been warmer then! And yet, no—for in October of this inclement, summerless year of grace 1924, I saw a great tree on a red brick wall in an old garden within a mile of Liberton, and its branches were laden with peaches that glowed red in the afternoon light.

Old Granton Castle—the real Royston, which was built in 1554—stands on a rock overhanging the shore. As we gaze through its empty windows, at the workmen who are gradually quarrying away the rock, there comes a sough of the Melvilles who first built it; or Henry VIII., whose raiding seamen burned it; of Sir Thomas Hope of Craigiehall, the Advocate of Charles I., who lived here when he wished to get a breath of purer air than that he could find at his house in the Cowgate.

Here, too, I can see ghosts: within this old shell of a castle which until recently was a considerable ruin: and down yonder, on the melancholy shore, where in the fading light an old woman is gathering coal-washings on the edge of the tide.

A messenger comes to the old house with news of a wreck in the Firth, and a cargo washed up on the shore below the gates. The Lady of Royston is soon dashing down the avenue with her company of young gallants—grand-nieces and nephews—at her heels. There, sure enough, on the rocks and sand are scattered books and workcases, knives, and curiosities such as children love. On another day the alarm is raised that the ruined castle is held by robbers. So an assault is planned. Treading softly, a search is made, the robbers are actually found, the fight begins, and after dispersing the enemy the wild men are seen scampering off through the gardens, leaving behind them untold treasures in the vaults and dungeons. And yet Lady John had arranged the whole ploy! The mysterious messengers, the robbers lurking in the castle—they were all her own servants. The wreck and the litter on the shore, or the seizing the robbers in the ruins, it was all stage-managed by herself! What a romantic way of giving the children presents— the litter on the shore and the treasures in the dungeons! I wonder if there are any old ladies left in the world to-day like Lady John Scott?

As I turn my back on the haunted house I can hear the cannon ball thumping on the floor of the Aurora drawing-room, and the clang of the bell at midnight as the Green Lady pulls the bell-rope in the courtyard, her ghostly garments dripping with the water of the well. But better far than

the sound of phantom cannon balls or clanging bells
is the music of Lady John's harp as she sits alone
in the white-panelled room, unaffrighted by ghosts
or bogles, singing one of her own songs.

> Like dew on the gowan lying
>   Is the fa' o' her fairy feet,
> And like winds in summer sighing
>   Her voice is low and sweet.
> Her voice is low and sweet,
>   And she's a' the world to me,
> And for bonnie Annie Laurie
>   I'd lay me doun and dee!

XXIII

INCHCOLM

OF all the islands of the Forth on which there are remains of ancient churches—the Bass Rock, the May Island, Fidra, Inchkeith and Inchcolm—the most interesting is Inchcolm, with its splendidly preserved ruins of an ancient abbey which stands on the site of the original Columban settlement. It may well be called "The Iona of the East," for not only are its religious traditions bound up with St Columba, who spread the gospel all over Scotland from the sacred isle of Iona, but on Inchcolm to-day we can look upon the best preserved ruins of any of the most ancient monastic establishments in Scotland.

The most precious building on Inchcolm is the Celtic Cell which was occupied by a Columban hermit. This Cell stands at the extreme north-west corner of the abbey garden, and with it is bound up the whole story of the origin of the Abbey. While Alexander I. was crossing the Forth some time during the first quarter of the twelfth century—he reigned from 1106 to 1124—he was caught in a violent storm and had to land for safety on the island of Inchcolm. He and his followers were maintained for three days by the hermit who was living in the little Columban Cell on the island, and who fed the King and his friends on shell-fish and the milk of his one cow. Alexander, in the year 1123, founded and endowed the Monastery of Inchcolm out of gratitude to God for his deliverance, and brought to the island some of the Augustinian canons who were living at the Monastery of Scone, which the King and his wife Sybilla had founded about ten years before. Little wonder that the Hermit's Cell was preserved as a relic by the later monks. These little cells or churches were erected in desolate spots and on islands all over the west of Scotland and elsewhere. The oldest specimens of Columban cells are to be found on one of the Garvelloch Isles to the south of Oban—Eilean na Naoimh—the Isle of Saints—and it is to the period of these ancient little cells and Columban churches that this Cell on Inchcolm belongs. It may be that its exact date will never be ascertained. But, although it measures only about sixteen feet long by four feet ten inches at the entrance and six feet at the east end, its style of building, its little window at the east end, its tiny ambry and its barrel roof all point to this Cell being one of the few relics of the Columban church which remains to us in the east of Scotland. The wonder is that it still remains, for although it has doubtless been frequently repaired, it has been used in later times both as a toolhouse and a pigsty.

The original Monastery has been added to at different dates, the Church being the oldest part, consisting of a nave and a central tower with a small northern transept. The newer Choir to the east has long since disappeared, and only the foundations can

P

be traced to-day. This choir was probably about one hundred feet long by about twenty feet in breadth. The Lady Chapel (a smaller church dedicated to the Blessed Virgin or " Our Lady," at the extreme end of the choir behind the altar) is here seen to open off the south side of the now demolished choir. It has been covered with a pointed barrel vault, and a portion of that still stands.

The cloisters at Inchcolm are very interesting, because they also form the ground storey of the domestic apartments round three sides of the cloister garth. The usual cloister was merely a covered walk which ran round the inner walls of the courtyard or garth or garden, from which doors led off to the various apartments. But, at Inchcolm, the ambulatory occupies the whole of the ground floor. This cool, dark walk, with its small round-headed windows, its stone seats in the deep recesses and its barrel roof, is very striking and primitive when a blazing sun sends slanting shafts of light across the gloom.

On the north side of the cloister garth ran the exposed wall of the nave and tower of the early church, which meant that the entrance to the church through the tower was exposed to the weather. So, at a later date, a covered way of the more usual type was erected by the monks along the north side of the cloister garth, and judging by the raglets in the walls which carried the sloping roof of this covered way, as well as by the foundations for a thin parapet wall, and five buttresses that still remain, it is easy to picture this lean-to addition.

Above the ambulatory were the monks' apartments; on the east side the dormitory, on the south side the refectory, and on the west side the novices' quarters. Access to these was got by means of the small stair, which is lighted by very small windows that look out on the cloister garth. In the refectory can still be seen the remains of the pulpit from which one of the monks read while the brothers were eating. A few steps in the thickness of the wall led up to it.

But the most considerable building, which opens off the eastern ambulatory, is the Chapter House— the building that was always incorporated in a monastic establishment or cathedral, and in which the chapter or clergy met to transact business. At Inchcolm the Chapter House is octagonal, and, like the choir, it seems to have been added towards the end of the thirteenth century. This date is confirmed in Inchcolm by the fact that Sir Alan Mortimer of Aberdour made large gifts of money and land to the Monastery in 1216, and purchased a right of burial in the Abbey Church. But when he died the monks who were conveying his body in a leaden coffin across the deep channel which runs between the Fife shore and the Sacred Isle, so mismanaged the barge that the coffin was lost overboard. Ever since, this channel has been known to seamen as Mortimer's Deep. So it was doubtless with Sir Alan's rich gifts that the later buildings at Inchcolm were erected in the thirteenth century. It is well known that little or no monastic building was carried on in Scotland from that time till the fifteenth century.

The octagonal Chapter House has a groined vault. The ribs spring from round shafts, and where they meet in a carved boss in the centre of the roof, there is a circular hole opening into the floor of the chamber above through which a lamp may have been lowered. The Chapter House has a fine doorway, a stone bench with a step running round the chamber, and three arched recesses with seats at the east end. Here sat the abbot, with the prior on his right and the sub-prior on his left. The chamber above is a rude and later erection, which was probably used as a warming room or study for the monks. It is said that the Scots historian—Walter Bower—who continued " Fordun's Chronicles of Scotland," may have added this study for his own use. He was the eleventh abbot and the greatest of them all. He was born at Haddington in 1385, and his reign at Inchcolm began in 1418. We can imagine the learned abbot sitting comfortably up there in his warm study working diligently at his history with the wild winter storms howling about him and his island monastery.

The large range of buildings across the entrance court from the Chapter House and the Lady Chapel were domestic offices. Here were the cellars, lighted by loop-holes, and above them five or six offices, two with large fireplaces and one with an oven in the angle.

The buildings on the north side of the tower and close to the sea may have been a guest or a lazar-house.

Between the monastery walls and the rocky height of the island on the west lay the garden. Over the garden wall to the south there is the monastery well —forty feet deep and built of stone. It is the only water supply on the island, and the water is cold and pleasant, though hard.

Beyond the garden on the grassy hilltop to the west lies an ancient gravestone—a fine specimen of a hog-backed stone which was used for a grave covering. It is a moving thought that this is the site of the ancient Danish graveyard of Inchcolm to which Shakespeare made reference in " Macbeth," Act I., Scene 2, in connection with the defeat of Sweno, King of Norway: —

> Sweno, the Norway's King, craves composition;
> Nor would we deign him burial of his men
> Till he disbursed at St. Colm's Inch
> Ten thousand dollars to our general use.

Here many human bones have been found, and the historians, Holinshed and Bellenden, mention, " Manie greit stanes graven with the armes of the Danes." We must remember that the Scandinavian Vikings harried and ruled our western seaboard and the isles from the end of the eighth century to the middle of the thirteenth century. Haco, the last of these rover kings, was defeated at the Battle of Largs in 1263. It will not astonish us, therefore, if this ancient burial mound on Inchcolm yields some interesting finds to the careful restorers.

Inchcolm, like Iona, was robbed, harried and burned many times. In 1335 it was harried by the English, who stole many of the precious things belonging to the monastery—chalices, censers, crosses, chandeliers, relics, vestments and images. It was attacked again in 1336. It was plundered and set on fire by the fleet of Richard II. in 1384. In 1543 the abbey seems to have been deserted, but after the Battle of Pinkie in 1547 it was occupied as

a centre for his fleet by that ruthless destroyer of
many of our finest border abbeys—Hertford, Duke
of Somerset.

It is quite apparent that the Abbey of Inchcolm
has been occupied as a private residence, and one
of the first tasks of the restorers was to remove
the partitions and plaster ceilings which have for
generations hidden the beauties of the original
building.

For centuries the abbey has been the property of
the Earls of Moray, and this is the story of how
it came into the hands of that great Scots family.
James Stuart of Beith was a favourite of James V.
and also of Pope Paul III. So he used his influence
with the King to get his son appointed as one of the
canons of Inchcolm. The son ultimately became
commendator of the abbey, and on the dissolution
of the monasteries was granted a feu-charter of the
lands of St Colme, and in 1581 a peerage under the
title of Lord Doune. On his death in 1590, the
island passed to his son, who married Elizabeth,
eldest daughter of the Good Regent Murray, and
who succeeded to the title and honours of his father-
in-law. He thus became the second Earl of Moray
—the " Bonnie Earl of Moray " of the ballad. Cast
your eye over yonder to the earl's lordly house of
Donibristle on the Fife shore, and you can picture
the whole circumstances of the ballad. The story
goes that the handsome earl was loved by Anne of
Denmark, King James's queen. He was suspected
by the King, who ordered Moray's greatest enemy,
the Earl of Huntly, to apprehend him. Huntly came
on Moray one night in his house at Donibristle,

ordered him to surrender, and on his refusing set fire to the house. Moray fought his way through his enemies and escaped to the seashore, but he was betrayed by the plumes of his helmet which had caught fire. Huntly, Gordon of Buckie, and others followed him, and in the struggle to capture him, Gordon of Buckie wounded the Bonnie Earl. When he felt himself dying, the earl exclaimed: " Ye hae spoiled a better face than your ane." Then Buckie, pointing a dagger at Huntly's breast, exclaimed with an oath, " You shall be as deep in this as I." So Huntly was forced to pierce the defenceless body.

> He was a braw gallant
>   And he played at the gluve;
> And the bonnie Earl o' Moray
>   He was the Queen's luve.

> O lang will his ladye
>   Look frae the castle Doune,
> Ere she see the Earl o' Moray
>   Come soondin' thro' the toon.

The old ballad expressed the popular feeling of indignation at the slaying of the Bonnie Earl.

What a centre of ecclesiastical history is this Island of Inchcolm! Alexander I., who founded the abbey, was a son of Queen Margaret, who, by her remarkable influence, won over the Celtic Church in Scotland to the Roman ritual. She is commemorated in Edinburgh by St Margaret's Chapel on the Castle Rock—the oldest building in the city—and by Dunfermline Abbey, where she had her shrine. King Edgar I., another of her sons, has his name enshrined in Port Edgar over yonder, now a naval

base.   Alexander I., not only founded this Abbey
of Inchcolm, but he gave lands to the churches
at Durham and Dunfermline and founded the
monastery at Scone.   King Davdi I., a third son of
Queen Margaret, will always be remembered as the
patron of the great Scots Cathedral builders.

The very name of Queensferry reminds us of the
mother of these three kings—for Margaret, who first
landed at St Margaret's Hope, founded hostels on
both sides of the Forth, and instituted a free ferry
for all pilgrims who wished to travel to the shrine
of St. Andrew in Fife.   At Abercorn over yonder,
which was once the northern limits of Northumbria,
Bishop Trumwin, who was appointed as Bishop of
the Picts, had his see in the seventh century. At
Culross, further up the shores of Fife, lived St Serf,
who succoured the Princess Thenew when she landed
from a coracle in which her father Loth, King of
Lothian, had set her adrift.

But greatest and best of all these early shrines
remaining to us to-day is this wonderful Island of
St Colm or Columba.

XXIV

CASTLE DUNGEONS

GHOSTS OF HISTORY AND ROMANCE

LITTLE wonder that the eye of every intelligent Scot is lifted with pride to the Castle on the Rock of Edinburgh. Yonder stands the most ancient monument of civilisation in this old grey city of the North. From the earliest times there was a fortress on that beetling crag. From the days of Queen Margaret, the Castle was a Royal residence. All these walls and towers and buildings, as they stand to-day, make a history of Scotland in stone, and if we could only pierce below the outer crust of masonry, what secrets might we not come upon!

In the year 1912 an official inspection of the older part of the castle by three wise men led to a very important discovery. In the coal cellar of the soldiers' canteen there was found a stone-vaulted recess, with a narrow slit or shot-hole. If that slit in the coal cellar could only be located on the outer walls below the Half-Moon Battery, other discoveries might follow. The work of excavation began from the battery itself on the 12th of August, and when our sportsmen were knocking over grouse on the moors of Scotland, the Government diggers were knocking through the little shot-hole. That was the beginning of the adventure. After a time they came to a stone floor, which was afterwards found to be the top of a vault. Having broken into the chamber below they gradually made their way to other underground chambers. But the excavation entailed an enormous amount of work. Hundreds of tons of earth and stone were taken to the surface in buckets. Now, a labyrinth of chambers and passages has been restored for those who are fortunate enough to get permission for a private view.

These underground rooms and passages belonged to the actual palace or tower of David II. (1329-1370). But to see them you have to descend on ladders or very rough steps to a depth of fifty-seven feet. Then, in the shadowy underworld, by the aid of lamp-light and electric bulbs, these old fourteenth-century chambers gradually emerge. At this point we come on the original city wall. Here also is the doorway, with its pointed head, which gave the only access to the Castle—a brave little gateway, with three checks, indicating that two doors opened outwards and one inwards. As we stand beneath the apex of the lintels, the ghosts of history flit past us, as Kings of Scots, with their nobles and soldier men pass in and out of the Castle. If it were permitted to spend a night alone down there, one might hear weird groans from the prisoners' quarters, and loud laughter from the hall of feasting. The eyes of a sentimental Scot might also see the gallant ghosts go hurrying by, and feel a draught of cold air on the cheek as they passed.

Standing now in a vaulted recess of the great wall, one can look through an oval-shaped loophole,

EDINBURGH AT SUNSET

which is carefully aligned to point directly down the High Street. Yet the building of the Half-Moon Battery had entirely covered up this ancient loophole, and the outer facing of that part of the battery wall had to be removed to expose permanently to view this very interesting relic. So, hidden history has now been revealed and to-day you may gaze on the City of Edinburgh through the loophole from the very heart of this long buried Tower of David.

It takes but a few minutes to climb up to the sunshine again. Crossing the old Palace Square to the west end of the Parliament Hall, we now descend the stair which leads to the later vaults and dungeons where, from 1756 to the beginning of the nineteenth century, many of the French prisoners were confined.

Robert Louis Stevenson has recaptured in " St Ives " something of the romance and tragedy which hang like a mist about these dark caverns. He must have visited them all, walking this battlement path, leaning perhaps on the stone parapet, and gazing on the glorious view towards his favourite Pentland Hills. He must also have sauntered in the little courtyard which was the only exercise ground of these homesick sons of France. Here are the ovens where they baked their bread. Stout chains still hang by the doors. Tremendous gratings and bars give the place an uncanny look. The very names which the French exiles carved on the stone walls can still be read near the door; one of them is *Charles d'Fobier de Calaise*, 1780. This rock-floored vault opening off the parapet walk, is the dungeon where the great Marquis of Argyle lay for months before his execution. The whole suite of dungeons calls up sorrows of the past, and our thoughts naturally keep turning to that gallant but sick-souled gentleman, Monsieur le Vicomte Anne de Keroual de Saint-Yves, otherwise the common prisoner who was called Champdivers.

In those days at certain hours the prison of this mediæval fortress was visited by the townfolks, who were curious to see the hapless captives and to buy some souvenir of their rude handiwork. I have beside me now a poor little wooden needle-case ornamented with beads, which one of those French prisoners made in that unhappy era when our great-grandfathers lived in daily terror of Bonaparte and his threatened invasion. There was another colony of French prisoners out yonder at Burdiehouse— the clachan which the Frenchmen called after their own home of Bordeaux. The douce lads of Lothian soon called it "Burdie," but to this day you will find the word *Bordeaux* cut on the stone face of a house at Burdiehouse.

On one of those red-letter visiting days St Ives first saw La Belle Flora from Swanston, and ever after that, he used to gaze with hungry eyes from the battlement walk towards Swanston Cottage, tucked away in a snug fold of the Pentlands— the home of this little lady of his dreams. Surely only the long-sighted eyes of love could see the smoke of the Swanston chimney from the Castle!

It is useless to-day to look for the shed where the famous duel with the pair of scissor blades took place. But it is easy in fancy to see that desperate fight between the punctilious Vicomte and that pothouse *soldat* Phillipe Goguelat, who had chosen to speak in a light way of La Belle Flora.

" I am a gentleman," said M. le Vicomte, " and I cannot bear to soil my fingers with such a lump of dirt . . . but . . . I promise you, Goguelat, you shall be dead to-night.

They had no weapons. But a pair of scissors and two tough wands were found. The scissors were unscrewed and each blade was lashed securely to a wand. The assailants were stripped to the shoes to avoid blood-stained clothing. The evening fell cloudy. The chill of night enveloped their bodies like a wet sheet. In the blackness of the shed the two men took up their positions.

" Allez! " said the Sergeant-Major.

Both lunged at the same time. M. le Vicomte felt a hot sting on the shoulder, while his own blade plunged below the girdle of Goguelat into a mortal spot.

Forty prisoners were confined in each vault. One night forty-nine escaped by cutting a hole at the foot of the parapet and lowering themselves by a rope to the ground; one fell and was killed; the others were captured. Doubtless on this incident Stevenson founded his story.

Here, on the battlement walk, is a stone shoot through which we can imagine St Ives and his slender French companions escaping on a night of sea fog, when the haar enveloped the Castle like a shroud. After dangling on his rope like a jumping-jack, he let go his hold and landed on his feet, astonished and mightily relieved. In the wet airs of the May night he scented the wild wallflower growing on the rock.

But St Ives and his fellow-prisoners were not the only ones to be lowered over the Castle Rock in a sea fog. Many years before St Ives escaped, a dead Queen was lowered over that ugly cliff. The body of Queen Margaret was secretly taken down the western side of the Castle Rock one foggy night in 1093 by her faithful friends. That incident might serve to show us that the Scots must have resented the Saxon influence of this wonderful woman; for immediately she died, Donald Bane, the dead King's younger brother, beseiged the Castle; and Margaret's friends, in their anxiety to fulfil her last wish, bore her body most perilously down the Rock, and so to Queensferry and across the Forth to her own church of the Holy Trinity at Dunfermline. " Some, indeed, tell us," adds Fordun in his chronicle, " that during the whole of that journey a cloudy mist was round about all this family, and miraculously sheltered them from the gaze of any of their foes."

All these things come to mind as we stand and gaze over the parapet on the storied city of our hearts, with its wondrous horizons of history and hills.

When we reach the Palace Square again, the eye does not seek the new war shrine so much as a little oblong stone in the ancient wall above a certain door, easy to find if you know where to look for it. If the story is a true one, there is behind that stone a coffin containing the remains of an infant prince of Scotland. King James VI., the wisest fool in Christendom, was never quite satisfied about his own legitimacy. Be that as it may, the story has it that Queen Mary's infant (the real James VI.) died, and, quite unknown to the Queen, the infant son of one of her ladies of the bedchamber—Lady Reres—was substituted for the Royal babe. And we know it as an historical fact that Lady Reres nursed the little King. If this be true, then Mary Queen of Scots was the last of the Stuarts. This fact, however, remains—that in 1830 a fire took place in the Royal apartments, and a tiny coffin, containing the remains of a child, was found built into the wall. The body had been wrapped in a shroud of silk and cloth of gold embroidered with initials, one of which was " I." But this may have been a holy vestment with the letters " I.H.S." upon it. The coffin was restored to the recess, and the wall was once more built up. It is a long story and the least said about it the better. A wise man without evidence neither affirms nor denies.

After all our collogues with these ghosts of the past, it is very pleasant to step into Queen Margaret's Chapel, which is the oldest building standing in Edinburgh to-day. No Queen did more than Queen Margaret to remodel the old Celtic Church in this land of her adoption. She persuaded her husband, Malcolm Canmore, to make the Castle of Edinburgh his chief residence; so from the reign of Malcolm and Margaret the Castle became for the first time really historic. Under the Queen's influence there was a renascence of culture in Scotland. Gold and silver vessels began to appear on the King's table, and this Royal mother set an example to her children and to her country. Here in this tiny chapel she would offer her prayers. So we stand to-day with reverent memories in this old Norman building, while the sunshine streams through the little stained-glass windows and lays the pavements in a mosaic of mystic reds and greens and blues.

XXV

CRAMOND AND BARNBOUGLE

NOWHERE does the spring come or the year die with greater beauty than at Cramond, that fairy creek on the Forth, with its picturesque huddle of houses, just within the new city boundary of Edinburgh.

To experience the surprise of Cramond, we must approach it by the shore-road from Granton. Coming along this path, the Forth, on a lown November day, at low tide can give us beauty to remember. Long level swathes of blue-grey mist: islands floating on the dim horizon, the shores of Fife beyond: restless sea-anger mellowed into a monotone of peace by the magic of distance. An autumn symphony in low, quiet tones. All along this shore the heights are well-wooded, and one mansion after another looks seaward through the trees, until we come to Cramond House itself. Indeed, this little bit of home country is dotted over with historic seats, each of which brings to mind families that have helped to make Scots history—Loch of Drylaw, Law of Lauriston, Howieson of Braehead, Elphinstone of Barnton, Inglis of Cramond, and Morton of Cammo.

Muirhouse, standing up there in the trees above the shore, was an old royal hunting box of the Scots kings . The barony was granted by Robert Bruce to Sir William Oliphant of Aberdalgie. In the year 1776 it was bought by a successful Scots merchant, William Davidson, who made a fortune in Holland. When he died he bequeathed it to his nephew, the Rev. Thomas Randall, D.D., of the Tolbooth Kirk, who took the name of Davidson, and his descendant was the late Archbishop of Canterbury.

Over the sea-wall at Nether Cramond you will see an old tower—the only remaining fragment of the summer palace of the Bishops of Dunkeld, and once a portion of the castle which stood near the old Roman Camp of Caer-almond. For there was here an important Roman military station, where three famous roads terminated—one leading westward to the Antonine Wall at Carriden, another going south, across the Borders by Watling Street, and a third going eastward to Inveresk. The well near-by may have been that of the Roman Camp.

The original church of Cramond was dedicated to St Columba, and the Bishops' palace was founded in the twelfth century when David I. granted the lands to the Bishopric of Dunkeld. For many years this was the chief Episcopal residence south of the Forth, and here Gawin Douglas penned some of his epistles. So it was called Bishops Cramond to distinguish it from Kings Cramond or Cramond Regis, which stood near the site of the modern house of Barnton.

An old, ancient place is Cramond. Step up the hill and in the kirkyard you may sit and remember in the silence that you are within the site of the Roman Camp, where three Roman altars and many

coins have been found.   How few wanderers along
this shore realise that in Cramond House, just over
the sea-wall, the great Polish musician Chopin was
at one time the guest of Lady Torphichen?   Here
he wandered in the woods, weaving melodious
dreams.   Here he must often have regarded the
ancient sundial with its thirty-three gnomons, and
sometimes he would lift his eyes to the islands.   In
this house did he play his nocturnes in the summer
gloamings?   Those perfect tone-poems which are so
like this same sea-sorrow, quiet and haunting, yet
relieved continually by ripples of joy.   I can see a
great bowl of roses in the low-ceiled room where
he played.   The moonlight steals in at the open
window and falls on the crimson blooms, until they
flame with a strange unearthly light.

Chopin, the Shelly of music, has been immortalised
in these words of Alfred Noyes: —

> Ah, remember how
> Poor Heine here in Paris leant
> Watching me play at the fall of day,
> And following where the music went
> Till that old cloud upon his brow
> Was almost smoothed away.

> " Do roses in the moonlight flame
> Like this and this? " he said and smiled,
> Then bent and hearkened till the dark
> Swelled with the silent sob a child
> Might utter o'er some dead friend's name.

> .   .   .   .   .   .

> " Do roses in the moonlight glow
> Like this and this? "

The old House of Cramond—Chopin playing in the dimly lit room—a bowl of red roses in the moonlight. It all comes before us as we sit alone by the old sea-wall and dream!

To get the real glamour of Cramond, there must be no trippers about, and you must stand solitary at the Cobble Ferry ,whistling for the drowsy ferryman to come down the wooden steps and take you across to the further shore. While you stand waiting you can sweep in all the wonders of Cramond with the eye; the island far out on the edge of the tide; the picturesque tumble of grey-white houses behind you, all thrown down in a heartsome huddle by that old architect, Time. In the Almond's sluggish estuary there are the remains of a wooden jetty where of old the little sloops discharged their iron ore for the smelting works up the stream, works which were linked with the name of Cadell.

Stepping now into the old boat, we stand looking about us while the ferryman sculls us across. The passage of the ferry is free to all who would cross to Dalmeny and continue the walk to Queensferry. But for those who would walk up the waterside there are many ancient things to discover: Peggy's Mill, and the old Brig of Cramond, where Jock Howieson met King James V. disguised as the Guid Man o' Ballengeich, and rescued him from some wandering gypsies who had attacked him. The path through the beautiful woods of Craigiehall will take you further up the stream to the Grotto Bridge. This part of the river is steeped in legendry and historic lore.

We are reminded of the Act of Parliament of the

year 1662, part of which runs thus: "That the
Bridge of Crawmond wes by publict order built for
the better passage of travellers betwixt Queinsferrie
and Leith and Edinburgh, yet notwithstanding
theirof, diverse persons haveing occasion to travell
that way doe not make use therof But come in a
privat way by the seaside which (being only at
first for the private use of the Lairds of Barnbougall
the petitioners authors) leads directly in by the gate
of the petitioners house of Barnbougall whereby he
is prejudged by the destroying and cutting of his
planting and breaking of this closures and trees
Lykas this gate is no publict hie way . . . and it
were hard that they should be tollerat to come so
neir his gates and destroy his enclosures . . .
Humbly therefor desireing order may be given for
stoping that passage and that the passangers may
either go to the bridge in the ordinar hie way or
other wayes some other way may be found out for
them." So the Act runs on and on—but the way
that was found out was the ferry. To-day the
ferry is kept open by Lord Rosebery. No charge is
made. Bundles or bags may not be carried across;
no one may cross from the village to Dalmeny after
6 p.m.; but any one may cross at a later hour from
Dalmeny to Cramond. So the bye-laws run.

On the Dalmeny side, the path along the shore
through the woods past Dalmeny House and Barnbougle Castle to Queensferry is one of the finest
walks near Edinburgh.

A few hundred yards from the ferry will bring
you to the Hunter's Craig, or Eagle Rock—a
craggy stone crowned with turf and whin, standing

on the sandy shore. Incised on the rock face is a remarkable carving of an eagle. This is said to be a relic of Roman times. The interesting sculpturing, which has been done at great labour, is now covered with a fine-mesh iron cage to prevent destruction.

The path continues round a headland—the Snabpoint—which brings us in full view of the great bay with the Drum Sands lying yellow and glistering in the afternoon sun. Dalmeny House stands there on its green lawns among the trees, and Barnbougle Castle crowns the further point. Surely no bay of such remote beauty lies so near the bounds of the city! Here at the head of the sands is Long Green, a row of cottages with their backs to the sea and their sunny garden fronts to the woodlands. How green is the old turf, and how merrily sings the Cockle Burn under the little bridge on its way to the sea! The little estuary is a sanctuary for seabirds in winter. The sands beyond the young firwood are rich with thousands of many-coloured shells. In spring and summer the woods are carpeted with flowers and in mid-winter the walk is beautiful. Barnbougle on the point draws us irresistably by its romantic situation and history.

The Moubrays who owned it came over with William the Conqueror in 1066 and were of pure Norman descent. Philip de Moubray was Lord of Barnbougle, Dalmenie, and Inverkeithing in the reign of Alexander II., and he died in the year 1221. The last of this ancient line died out with Sir Robert Moubray, who sold the property in 1615 to Sir Thomas Hamilton, Lord Advocate, afterwards created Earl of Haddington. This earl's grandson sold the estate to Sir Archibald Primrose, who was created Earl of Rosebery and Lord Dal-menie in 1703, and to this family the lands still belong. A former Primrose pulled down (for family reasons) the original building and was nearly successful in razing it to the ground. An appeal was made on behalf of the Forth fisher-folk and the sailors, to leave the remaining walls standing as a guide to navigators on the Forth. This original part was built into the north wall and carefully preserved by Lord Rosebery when he restored the Castle in 1880. In his time, no one was allowed within the rails of the policy which now surrounds Barnbougle.

The name Barnbougle is variously explained. In a little old book on the district written about seventy years ago there is a legend worth repeating. The writer suggests that Barnbougle means the Baron's Bugle, and the tale is as follows: —

In the time of the Crusades there lived here a lonely man named Sir Roger. He left these lands for Palestine, where, as a red-cross knight, he fought against the foes of Christ. Before leaving he kept vigil in the Church of St Adamnan at Dalmenie and kissed his crozier-hilted sword as he prayed for the good of the Brotherhood. He then went down to the point to board his little ship when lo! his favourite hound appeared and wailed so dismall looking up pitifully the while to his master's face, that Sir Roger was constrained to take the hound with him. So the knight and his dog together sailed for Syria. For years Sir Roger fought as a

Crusader. One dark night in the old tower by the
Forth, the sound of a bugle rang through the
keep, and out on the point where Sir Roger had
embarked a death-wail arose on the winds as a
ghostly hound bayed. It was Sir Roger's weird,
for at that moment, he lay dead on the battle-field
with his faithful brach beside him!

> And ever when barnbougle's lords
> Are parting this scene below,
> Come hound and ghost to that haunted coast,
> With death notes winding slow.

Here, at least, we have a meaning for Hound
Point, further along the shore, in the crusading
baron, the ghostly bugle, and the legend of Barnbougle Castle. So, with the sound of a phantom
bugle in our ears we continue our way westwards,
past the Wishing Well and the fisherman's lonely
cottage, and eventually reach The Hawes Inn at
Queensferry.

One more rare sight ere we return to town.
Stepping up the Hawes Brae for a mile, we come
to a point where the road cuts through the high
ground. On the right hand side there is an old
quarry hole or stone depot. Climbing up the
steep bank above the depot we come on the
Pilgrim's Stone—a large square double-stepped
foundation with a deep square hole in the topmost
platform. This hole is filled in now with a loose
upright stone; but centuries ago a great Cross or
Calvary must have stood here; for at this point,
the pilgrims coming north to the shrine at Dunfermline caught their first glimpse of that holy

THE PILGRIM STONE

fane of Saint Margaret, who made her Queen's
Ferry free to all pilgrims.   The trees obscure the
view to-day, but as we stand and gaze northward,
the centuries vanish and we are chanting a Bene-
dictus with many a travel-stained monk in whose
eyes there is the rapt look of one who at last sees,
though still far off, the end of his quest and would
go over to worship.

GLOSSARY

Appleringie, southernwood
Aught, passessed. *Whase aught this hoose?* Who owns this house
Auld-farrant, sagacious, shrewd

Bein, well-to-do
Bield, shelter
Bigging, building
Bing, heap; *blaes bing,* waste-heap at colliery, etc.
Birk, birch-tree
Bittock, little bit
Bocht, bought
Bogie, bogey, goblin
Bools, marbles
Brach, sport dog
Brock, badger
Bucht, sheep-fold
Buirdly, large, well-made
But and ben, house of two rooms

Caller, fresh
Cantrip, freakish behaviour
Chap, knock at the door
Chittering, shivering
Claes, clothes
Clanjamfrey, company, mob, gang
Clarty, dirty, muddy
Cleuch, small glen or hollow with steep banks
Cloor, blow or knock
Cloot, cloth
Collogue, confidential talk
Coup-cart, trouser-seat
Couthie, kindly, comfortable

Divot, thin oblong turf
Doer, estate manager
Dooms, very, absolutely
Douce, sober, modest

Dour, obstinate, hardy
Dowie, sad, dreary
Dreich, wearisome
Duds, clothes
Dwam, swoon, dream

Ettling, aspiring, striving after

Ferlie, a wonder
Flukie, small flounder
Fornent, opposite to
Freit, superstitious notion

Gangrel, vagrant
Gentrice, well-born
Gey, worthy of notice
Girning, snarling
Gurly, stormy, bleak

Haar, fog
Happit, covered from the cold
Haud, hold
Heicht, height
Hinmost, last
Hirsel, flock, or sheep holding
Holm, houm, rich flat ground beside a river
Hoolet, owl
Horse-couper, horse-dealer
Hottering, boiling slowly
Howe, used both for a small hill and a hollow
Howf, haunt

Ilka, each every

Jeddart, Jedworth, Jedburgh
Jick, jink

Kail, broth
Knowe, little hill
Kye, cows

251

Laigh, low
Lallan, lowland
Lampin', taking long steps or bounds
Lintie, linnet
Lown, calm
Lum, chimney

Marl, twisted colours
Moul, mould
Muckle, much

Namely, famous
Nickle, knuckle; *nickle deid*— in playing marbles—have the knuckles dead on the ground
Norie, whim

On-ding, downpour
Orraman, man employed to do odd jobs
Ower, over, across
Owercome, refrain of a song
Oxee, tit-mouse

Pawkie, sly, shrewd
Pech, breathe hard, pant
Piece, piece of bread
Ploy, employment, frolic
Plunk, propel marble with thumb; *plunk them fu'*, play strong
Pock, bag

Rax, reach
Reek, smoke
Reiver, robber
Rigmarole, long-winded story
Rowth, plenty

Sair Sanct, costly or extravagant saint.

Serk, shirt
Siccar, secure, certain
Sib, related to
Skew, gable slope
Sklent, slant
Skliddery, difficult to climb because of small stones
Sklim, climb
Skrunt, scrubby trees or bushes
Smoor, smother
Snell, keen, severe
Soondin', noise of galloping horse
Sough, sigh, rumour
Speil, climb
Stey, difficult, steep
Stound, ache
Strae, straw
Stravaig, wander
Streikit, stretched, laid out
Stunk, stake in game of marbles
Swither, hesitate

Taigle, hinder
Tearlach Og, young Charlie (Gaelic)
Theekin', thatch
Thirl, to thrall, enslave
Thrum, loose thread
Troke, bargain, business
Tousy, disordered
Tulzie, fight, scrap

Unco, unusual, very
U.P., United Presbyterian

Weird, prediction of death
Whaup, curlew

Yearthen, earthen
Yett, gate
Yowes, sheep

Morven

Mull of the Mountains

Appin

Benderloch

The Wild Bounds

Kilm

Oban

The Real Argyle

Loch Awe

Inverary

L. Katrine

Loch Lomond

St.

Isle of Jura

Isle of Islay

Isle of Cowal

Knapdale

Bute

Greenock

Dumbarton

Renfrew

Cunningham

Cantyre

Isle of Arran

Kyle

River

River Doon

Ayr

STINCHAR WATER

GIRVAN WATER

Carrick

L. Doon

R. Finches

Wigton

The Rhinns

Luce Bay

Water of Cree

Border By-ways and Lothian Lore